SPOOKY

Campfire Tales

SPOOKY
Campfire Tales

*Hauntings, Strange Happenings,
and Supernatural Lore*

RETOLD BY S. E. SCHLOSSER

ILLUSTRATED BY PAUL G. HOFFMAN

FALL RIVER PRESS

New York

FALL RIVER PRESS

New York

An Imprint of Sterling Publishing
387 Park Avenue South
New York, NY 10016

Text design by Lisa Reneson

ISBN 978-1-4351-4379-1

Manufactured in the United States of America

2 4 6 8 10 9 7 5 3 1

www.sterlingpublishing.com

For my family: Dave, Dena, Tim, Arlene, Hannah, Emma, Nathan, Ben, Deb, Gabe, Clare, Jack, Chris, Karen, and Davey.

Also for Brenda and Dan, and for the Draper family, with whom we have spent many an evening around the campfire.

* * *

Contents

PART TWO: POWERS OF DARKNESS AND LIGHT

Introduction

The fire was blazing nicely, warming up the chilly air as the guitar players tuned up with the fiddle. The kids were running back and forth between the campfire and the lake edge, shouting their general joy in living as dusk settled over the clearing. I leaned back in my camp chair, content just to listen as the musicians began playing old folk songs and hymns and anything else that caught their fancy.

The view from my seat was spectacular; several miles of lake rippled softly under a dark-blue sky, surrounded by wooded mountains. A few large rocks burst forth from the water near the center of the inlet, atop which drowsed a pair of Canada geese whom we had dubbed Bob and Lorraine on the first day of vacation. From somewhere to the north, a loon called its wild, lonely cry, and my niece answered it from the lakeshore, sounding like a close cousin.

Marshmallows and chocolate and graham crackers appeared as if by magic. I hooted with laughter as my two-year-old nephew tried to figure out how to roast a marshmallow with the assistance of his older cousin. As I watched the marshmallow roast, a niece handed me a Styrofoam cup steaming with hot chocolate—the perfect drink for a campfire. And night slowly fell over the scene, as eager musicians brought out their flashlights so they could read the words of their songs, and tired children collapsed into chairs or crawled into laps.

When darkness fell completely and the lake was a shadowy mirror against blue-black hills with a gazillion stars blooming overhead, the grown-ups started calling out song titles, hoping to hear old favorites they remembered from campfires long ago.

"Oh, Danny-boy, the pipes, the pipes are calling," I sang softly as the violin played. This plaintive melody was quickly replaced with upbeat tunes remembered from childhood as each new song sparked another memory. The kids sat quietly, listening to the adults sing and chiming in when they knew a number.

All too soon, the fire burnt down to ashes, the instruments were put away, and another farewell campfire was but a memory.

At this latest campfire, I was given a break and allowed to be entertained, rather than to do the entertaining, a rare occurrence for the author of spooky folklore books. Far more often, I find myself on my feet, moving around the blazing fire as I ask my listeners, "What kind of story would you like to hear tonight?"

"A scary story!" is the inevitable reply. I look around the campfire, seeing some faces brightly lit by the fire, some in shadow. All the eyes are eager, and several people sit forward in anticipation. A sense of mischief overwhelms me. Well, they asked for it . . .

"Now old Uncle Phil was a tall *scarecrow* of a fellow," I begin, gesturing broadly to indicate how tall Uncle Phil was, "who was jumpier than a grasshopper." I leap backward to demonstrate the grasshopper effect and almost knock over my chair. All talking has ceased at this juncture, and every eye is fixed upon me as I tell one of my favorite folktales: *Turnabout Is Fair Play.*

My audience starts to chuckle as the practical jokes played on Uncle Phil get funnier and more elaborate. When Uncle Phil dies, they grow silent. And when the ghost of Uncle Phil returns and begins to play practical jokes on his former tormentors, the air gets tense with excitement laced with just the teensiest bit of fear. This story is scary but safe, the way I like my ghost stories. (Otherwise, how would I sleep at night?)

At the climax of the story, the ghost of Uncle Phil tears off his scarecrow mask and shouts "Gotcha!" My shout of triumph at this juncture is eclipsed only by the screams of my audience. I swear they jump nearly a foot out of their chairs every time I reach this part of the tale. Afterward, my listeners sigh in relief and begin chattering about how scared they were (or weren't), and about how much they liked (or disliked) the story. Everyone has a reaction; most of them are positive. And everyone wants to hear more. Of course, I have only just gotten warmed up!

I know hundreds of ghost stories and spooky tales, far more than could ever be included in one book. For this collection, I have assembled some of my very favorite folktales. All of them can be read aloud around the campfire, and some I use over and over again whenever a storyteller is called for. *Tailypo* is perhaps my favorite spooky story of all time. Why? Because I love the way it feels to say "scratch, scratch, scratching." That "tch" sound grinds over the tongue and gives me goosebumps each time I say it! And of course, unlike the ending of the Uncle Phil story, the ending of *Tailypo* leaves me shivering.

If you are looking for some funnier spooky stories, try *I Can't Get In,* in which a testy skeleton gives a lecture to a boy who is sitting disrespectfully upon his grave; or *Never Mind Them Watermelons,* in which the unlucky Sam Gibb takes a bet with a blacksmith to stay overnight in a haunted cabin.

Want to scare your audience? Then *Dark Passenger* and *One Last Head* are the stories for you. A vampire stalks the crew of a ship crossing the Great Lakes in the former, and the specter of an insane killer drives his son mad in the latter.

Have you ever heard someone practicing the piano over and over again until you wanted to scream? Then you'll relate to the narrator of *Playin' Piano!* And if you're looking for some creepy tales of victims avenging themselves after death, try *Vengeance* and *Bloody Bones.*

If you want a few stories that will entertain the kids but still let them sleep after your campfire, try *Shadow Train* or *Ghost Handprints.* In the first, a ghost train picks up a passenger in the middle of the desert; in the second, ghostly children save the lives of a stranded couple.

Perhaps the capstone of the collection—not to mention the most popular piece on my Web site Americanfolklore.net—is the story of *Bloody Mary,* the witch whose curse is said to haunt every darkened mirror. This curse is still whispered at sleepover parties all over America. The retold story in this collection is narrated by a blacksmith who had a personal encounter with the witch.

I could go on and on about every story in *Spooky Campfire Tales*, but perhaps it is best if you read them for yourself. They run the gamut from funny to terrifying. I hope you will find something suitable to read aloud to every type of audience you may encounter around your own campfires.

Don't forget to bring the marshmallows!

— Sandy Schlosser

PART ONE
Ghost Stories

1

The Fifty-Cent Piece

The young couple departed much later than they expected from their cousin's house. They were still miles from home when dusk fell over the narrow, windy road they traveled. The horses were tired, the night was chilly, and there was no inn anywhere in sight. The husband clicked his tongue thoughtfully, a sure sign that he was getting worried. His young wife laid a hand on his arm and suggested that they seek out a house and ask for shelter for the night. Her husband considered this proposal for a moment, then smiled and acquiesced. As they traveled the long, bumpy road that led from Massachusetts to New York, they started watching for a house.

It was the husband who spied a light through the trees just when his wife had resigned herself to a cold night spent in a parked carriage. He turned their horse onto a narrow dirt road leading up a hill. A pleasant little house stood at the crest. The light was shining cheerfully from the windows, illuminating a pretty, well-kept yard.

Their carriage was spotted as they drove up the hill, and an old man and his wife met the couple at the door. The old folks were in nightclothes and had obviously been about to go to bed, but their welcome was warm. The elderly couple introduced themselves as Mr. and Mrs. Brown. The old wife took the young woman by the arm, tutting briskly over her cold hands.

"You'll catch your death out in this cold, damp air," Mrs. Brown exclaimed. "Papa, throw some more wood on the fire."

She whisked the young folks inside the cozy house and settled them into comfortable chairs close to the fireplace before the young husband could explain the reason for their unexpected visit.

As old man Brown built up the fire, the young man asked if they might rent a room for the night, since there was no inn nearby and they were still many miles from home.

"Rent? Don't be ridiculous," exclaimed Mrs. Brown. "You must be our guests!" She ignored the young couple's protests and bustled out of the room to get them some hot food. Feeling overwhelmed by such kindness, the young man and his pretty wife supped on the good meat and cakes placed before them and chatted merrily with their host and his wife.

After the impromptu dinner, old man Brown and his wife escorted the weary couple to their room. As they parted for the night, the young husband once again volunteered to pay for their lodgings. Mrs. Brown stiffened and shook her head reproachfully at the young man, and her husband said: "Nay, lad, 'tis but a small service we offer you. Keep your money and buy something pretty for your young lady."

The travelers woke early and tiptoed out of the cozy house. The young husband hesitated a moment, and then left a shiny fifty-cent coin in the center of the kitchen table where the old couple could not miss it. Then he hitched up their horse, and they went on their way. After several miles, they came to Spiegletown in New York. Spotting an inn, they went inside and purchased breakfast.

The innkeeper was a jolly fellow who came over to talk to them as they ate. When the husband mentioned the nice old couple who had given them lodging the previous night, the innkeeper turned pale.

"Where did you say that house was?" the innkeeper asked. The husband described the location in detail.

"You must be mistaken," said the innkeeper. "I know that place. That house was destroyed three years ago in a fire that killed the entire Brown family."

"I don't believe it," the husband said flatly. "Mr. and Mrs. Brown were alive and well last night."

After debating the matter for a few minutes, the couple and the innkeeper drove their carriage back out of town toward the old Brown place. The ground was quickly covered in bright sunshine, and the wife soon recognized the place where they had turned off the main road the night before. To her surprise, the narrow lane was overgrown with weeds, and dead branches crackled under the carriage wheels as they turned into it. She glanced uneasily at her husband and saw that he was equally disturbed. The track had not looked this way when they left earlier that morning. The carriage climbed the hill to the crest, and as they entered the yard, they saw a burned-out shell of a house that had obviously not sheltered anyone for a long time.

THE FIFTY-CENT PIECE

"This cannot be right," the wife exclaimed, climbing down out of the carriage and walking toward the blackened ruin.

"This is the Brown place," the innkeeper said.

"This is not where we stayed last evening," the husband insisted, slipping from the driver's seat to join the innkeeper on the ground. "I must have mistaken the direction."

And then the wife gave a terrified scream and swayed. Her husband leapt forward and caught her in his arms as she crumbled to the ground in a dead faint. Searching for the cause of her fright, the husband looked into the ruins and saw a burnt table with a shiny fifty-cent piece lying in the center, just where he had left it.

2

Ghost Handprints

My wife, Jill, and I were driving home from a friend's party late one evening in early May. It was a beautiful night with a full moon. We were laughing and discussing the party when the engine started to cough and the emergency light went on. We had just reached the railroad crossing where, according to local legend, a school bus full of children had stalled on the tracks right in front of an oncoming freight train. Everyone onboard the bus had been killed, and the ghosts of the children were reported to haunt this intersection, protecting people from danger.

Not wanting a repeat of the train crash, I hit the gas pedal, trying to get our car safely across the tracks before it broke down completely. But the dad-blamed car wouldn't cooperate. It stalled in the dead center of the railroad tracks.

Suddenly the railroad signals started flashing, and a bright light appeared a little way down the track, bearing down on our car. I turned the key and hit the gas pedal again, trying to get the car started.

"Hurry up, Jim! The train's coming," my wife began to panic.

GHOST HANDPRINTS

I immediately broke out into a sweat and tried the engine again. Nothing.

"We have to get out!" I yelled to Jill, reaching for the door handle.

"I can't," she shouted desperately. She was struggling with her seatbelt. We'd been having trouble with it recently. She'd been stuck more than once, and I'd had to help her get it undone.

I threw myself across the stick shift and fought with the recalcitrant seatbelt. My hands were shaking, and sweat poured down my body as I felt the rumble of the approaching train. It had seen us and was whistling sharply. I risked a quick glance over my shoulder. The engineer was trying to slow down, but he was too close to stop before he hit us. I redoubled my efforts.

Suddenly, the car was given a sharp shove from behind. Jill and I both gasped. I fell into her lap as the car started to roll forward, slowly at first, then gaining speed. The back end cleared the tracks just a second before the train roared past. As the car rolled to a stop on the far side of the tracks, the engineer stuck his head out the window of the engine and waved a fist, doubtless shouting something nasty at us for scaring him.

"Th—that was close!" Jill gasped as I struggled upright. "How did you get the car moving?"

"I didn't," I said. "Someone must have helped us."

I jumped out of the door on the driver's side and ran back to the tracks to thank our rescuer. In the bright moonlight, I searched the area, looking for the person who had pushed our car out of the path of the train. There was no one there. I called out several times, but no one answered. After a few minutes' struggle with her seatbelt, Jill finally freed herself and joined me.

"Where is he?" she asked.

"There's no one here," I replied, puzzled.

"Maybe he's just shy about being thanked," Jill said. She raised her voice. "Thank you, whoever you are!" she called.

The wind picked up a little, swirling around us, patting our hair and shoulders like the soft touch of a child's hand. I shivered and hugged my wife tightly to me. We had almost died tonight, and I was grateful to be alive.

"Yes, thank you," I repeated loudly to our mystery rescuer.

As we turned back to our stalled vehicle, I pulled out my cell phone, ready to call for a tow truck. Beside me, Jill stopped suddenly, staring at the back of our car.

"Jim, look!" she gasped.

I stared at our vehicle. Scattered in several places across the back of our car were glowing handprints. They were small handprints; the kind that adorn the walls of elementary schools all over the country. I started shaking as I realized the truth: Our car had been pushed off the tracks by the ghosts of the schoolchildren killed at this very location.

The wind swept around us again, and I thought I heard an echo of childish voices whispering, "You're welcome," as the wind patted our shoulders and arms. Then it died down, and the handprints faded from the back of the car.

Jill and I clung together for a moment in both terror and delight. Finally, I released her, and she got into the car, while I called the local garage to come and give us a tow home.

3

The White Lady

I must have tried on ten outfits before I finally decided what I was going to wear on my very first date with Jeff. I had been on the phone all afternoon with one friend after the other, discussing colors, accessories, nail polish, and all the other style essentials that I normally don't think about, since I consider myself an intellectual rather than a fashion plate. But that was before I was asked out by the most popular boy in school.

I went out on the front porch to polish my toenails. I was a third of the way through when a familiar shadow blocked the warm spring sunshine for a moment. I didn't even look up.

"What is it now, Stan?" I asked wearily. My neighbor since birth shuffled his way into the wicker chair next to mine.

"Listen, Jamie, is it true Jeff is taking you on a picnic to Durand-Eastman Park?"

Good grief, I thought. Jeff had just made the final arrangements with me half an hour ago. I had, of course, immediately phoned my best friend, Diane, and told her the news. Assuming it took Diane at least ten minutes to call all our other friends, and then another ten minutes for them to call their friends, that would mean that the news must have reached Stan within twenty-five minutes after I hung up with Jeff. That had to be some kind of gossiping record, I concluded, looking over at Stan.

Stan looks a bit like a sandy-haired scarecrow. He's 6 feet 2 inches and naturally plays basketball, but outside the court he appears a bit awkward, as if he has two left feet. Stan is also an intellectual, like me. I consider him a good friend, except for his irritating habit of asking me to go out with him at least once a month. I mean, I like Stan, but just as a friend.

"We are going to the park," I answered his question. "Why?"

"I think you should ask Jeff to take you to the movies," Stan said. "The park is a bad idea."

"What do you mean, a bad idea?" I asked suspiciously. Now what was Stan up to? Was he trying to break my date with Jeff?

"Come on, Jamie, even you must have heard about the White Lady," Stan said.

I stared at Stan incredulously for a moment, and then started to laugh. "For a second there, I thought you were serious," I gasped. "The White Lady! For goodness sake, Stan, no one believes that old story!"

Stan frowned and I stopped laughing. He couldn't be serious! But apparently he was.

The White Lady was the most famous ghost around Rochester (she haunts the Rochester suburb Irondequoit, just to the north). In the early 1800s, the White Lady and her daughter were supposed to have lived on the land where Durand-Eastman Park now stands. Then one day, the daughter disappeared. Convinced that the girl had been harmed and killed by a local farmer, the mother, accompanied by her two German shepherds, searched the marshy lands day after day for her child's body. She never found a trace of her daughter and finally, in her grief, committed suicide. Her faithful dogs pined for their mistress after her death, and soon followed her to the grave. The mother's spirit returned to continue the search for her child. People say that on foggy nights, the White Lady and her dogs rise from Durand Lake. Together, they roam through the park, looking for the missing daughter and seeking vengeance against men. Any man who catches the ghost's eye had best beware, for the White Lady and her dogs are killers. Or at least that's the version of the story I heard at school.

"Come on, Stan. You don't really believe there is a White Lady," I said. "I mean, ghosts? Please!"

"I would still feel much better about the whole thing if you and Jeff went to the movies," Stan said stubbornly.

"I'm touched by your concern," I said sarcastically. "But I am sure we will be just fine. Now, I have to go change. Jeff is picking me up at 6:30."

I left Stan sitting morosely on my porch and went to prepare for my date.

Jeff pulled into my driveway promptly at 6:30 P.M. in his yellow convertible. He was polite and polished with my parents, assuring them he would have me home by curfew, and then he tucked me into the front seat next to him. I could smell fried chicken coming from the picnic basket.

Stan was sitting in a rocker on his porch, watching us as we drove off. Jeff nodded stiffly to him; Stan nodded back.

"I didn't know you lived next door to Stan," Jeff said.

"All my life," I said. Just then my cell phone rang. I answered it, and Stan said, "Tell Jeff that you want to go to the movies."

"Give me a break, Stan," I said, and hung up.

Jeff glanced over at me. "What did Stan want?" he asked.

"Stan thinks we should go to the movies instead of to the park," I explained. "He thinks the White Lady will come and get us if we go there."

Jeff laughed. "I didn't think Stan was so superstitious!" he said. "Or is he jealous?" he asked, glancing at me again.

"I don't know!" I said impishly. "Maybe!"

We laughed and talked all the way to the park. Jeff parked the car in the lot next to Lake Ontario, and we crossed the street to what he called "the White Lady's castle," which overlooks both Lake Ontario and the smaller Lake Durand, a lovely, tree-shrouded lake directly across the street from Lake Ontario. We climbed up the stairs and spread the blanket out on the grassy spot at the top, behind the cobblestone wall. I unpacked the picnic basket, and we sat munching fried chicken and comparing notes about our teachers. Then Jeff started making some sly, rather uncomplimentary remarks about Stan, which I didn't appreciate. I guess he didn't like Stan calling me and telling me not to go to the park. When I didn't respond to his witticism, Jeff changed the subject, embarking upon a monologue of his athletic exploits, which, frankly, bored me to tears. Jeff was really cute, but I prefer my guys to have a bit more modesty than Jeff was displaying.

It was dusk when I heard a crashing noise and a familiar muffled cursing coming from the trees behind us. I knew at once that it was Stan. Jeff looked around.

"What was that?" he asked lazily.

"Just some kids fooling around," I said, glaring at Stan, who retreated behind a tree. Go home, I mouthed at him and turned to smile at Jeff.

"Fooling around, eh?" Jeff said, giving me a wicked grin. "Sounds like fun!"

Jeff leaned toward me, and I jumped up and walked over to the right side of the wall to look out at Durand Lake. I wasn't going to kiss that vain bore, even to get back at Stan.

To my right, the mist was rising off Durand Lake and the light was growing dim. I could see Stan scrambling down the hill toward the lake as silently as he could. He looked upset, but it served him right for following me on my date. Then I heard a step behind me and Jeff slid his arms around my waist.

"What's the matter, Jamie? Are you playing hard to get?" he asked, nuzzling my neck.

I was watching the mist over the lake, which was swirling strangely. I blinked a few times and suddenly realized that I was seeing a beautiful woman solidifying before my eyes. Two smaller swirls beside her became German shepherds. The White Lady was watching Stan, who had just reached the road at the bottom of the hill. She did not look happy to see him. Stan did not look happy to see her either. For a moment, my neighbor and the ghost stared at one another. The dogs at her side bristled, baring their teeth at him. Then the ghost gestured to the dogs and they ran toward Stan. Stan hightailed it back up the slope as fast as he could go, the ghost dogs snapping at his heels. The White Lady's face transformed from that of a beautiful woman to that of a haggard witch. She started rising up from the surface of the lake, following the crashing sounds Stan was making as he ran up the hill.

"Don't be so shy," Jeff said, nuzzling my hair.

Just then, the White Lady caught a glimpse of me and Jeff cuddled up next to the wall. Stan was forgotten in an instant. I stiffened as the ghost, accompanied by her two dogs, started rushing toward us! Feeling me tense, Jeff looked up and saw the White Lady for the first time. He let go of me so fast that I fell against the wall. Jeff didn't even notice. He was too busy stumbling backward, gasping swear words, and falling over the picnic basket. I was frozen to the spot, praying that the stories about the White Lady were true, and that she protected females rather than killing them. The White Lady ignored me completely. I ducked as she sailed right over my head in a rush of freezing cold air. She was aiming for Jeff with a look of murder on her face, and Jeff didn't wait around. He flew around the wall and half-ran half-stumbled down the stairs, the White Lady on his heels.

I grabbed my cell phone and ran to the top of the steps just as two enormous, semitransparent German shepherds flew across the wall in pursuit of their mistress. I jumped out of their way and watched Jeff running across the road and down the hill toward Lake Ontario, the White Lady and her dogs in hot pursuit. I flipped open my cell phone, started to dial 9-1-1, then paused. The emergency staff would think I was a kook if I reported a malicious ectoplasm chasing my date into the lake. Who do you call when a ghost gets out of hand?

Jeff plunged into the lake and submerged. The White Lady floated over the place he disappeared, looking very upset and very determined.

THE WHITE LADY

Just then, I heard someone call my name. I turned around. Stan was at the edge of the woods, looking nervously at the ghosts hovering over the water. I was relieved to see him in one piece.

"Are you okay?" he called.

I nodded and waved him into the woods, afraid of what the White Lady might do if she saw him. Then I turned back to see what was happening to Jeff.

The White Lady was floating back and forth over the water discontentedly. There was no sign of Jeff. *He has to be making some kind of world record for holding his breath,* I mused. The White Lady turned slowly toward shore and started floating up, up, up to the overlook until she drew even with me. The ghost and I looked at each other for a moment. Finally, she nodded to me, her face once again beautiful. Then she beckoned to the dogs, and together they floated out over Durand Lake, growing dimmer and dimmer until they had faded away completely.

I turned back toward Lake Ontario and saw Jeff's head come bursting out of the water. He gasped desperately for air, looking around for the White Lady.

"Jeff!" I shouted. "She's gone!"

I started running down the stairs as Jeff raced from the lake. He looked neither right nor left. He just ran straight up the bank and into the parking lot, leaped into his car, and roared away. I stopped halfway down the steps, my mouth hanging open. *He left me,* I thought blankly. That no-good rotter left me alone with the ghost and her two dogs.

It was almost completely dark now. I walked slowly back up the stairs, wondering what to do. Mechanically, I gathered up the remains of the picnic and folded up the blanket. Then I flipped open my cell phone and dialed a familiar number.

"Yes?" Stan answered on the first ring.

"Did you see that?" I demanded into my phone.

"I saw that," Stan said, keeping his voice neutral.

"He left me! He didn't even try to find out if I was all right," I said indignantly. "Would you give me a ride home?"

"I'd be happy to," said Stan. He hesitated a moment and then said, "You know, there's still time to catch a late movie."

I thought about it. On the one hand, there was handsome, popular Jeff who had left me to the mercy of the White Lady. On the other hand, there was my faithful Stan, who had been chased by the White Lady's dogs and had come back to make sure I was all right. Of course, this whole scene might have been an elaborate plot by Stan to get a date with me. Still, the ghosts had seemed real.

"Okay," I said into the phone.

There was a stunned pause, and then Stan said, "I'll bring the car to the bottom of the stairs." He hung up.

I could hear his whoop of utter happiness all the way across the park. A moment later, I heard a car engine start, and I knew he was on his way to pick me up. I grabbed the picnic basket and started down the stairs, grinning from ear to ear, to meet Stan.

4

Playin' Piano

Dah-dah-dum-dum-BLAT!

Charlie winced when his wife hit the wrong note on the piano for the thirty-second time that day. He knew it was the thirty-second time because he'd kept count as he went about his daily chores: cleaning the lighthouse, checking the supplies, mending the rowboat.

Charlie and his wife, Myrtle, lived on a small island off the coast of Maine. Charlie was the lighthouse keeper, and he worked hard to keep everything up-to-date, spankin' clean, and in perfect order. No ships were going to wreck on the local reef while he was in command of the lighthouse. Myrtle kept house and made crafts to sell at the local onshore market during their once-a-month trip into town.

Charlie and Myrtle had been married for almost ten years, and generally got along quite happily together, despite having no children. After she lost the first two, the doctor had told Myrtle that she wouldn't be able to have any more. Myrtle had taken the news stoically and had refused to adopt a child from the orphanage when Charlie proposed the idea. Still, Charlie suspected she really did feel the lack of motherhood in her life, and that it was probably the cause of her latest obsession.

Charlie blamed himself, really. He should never have taken Myrtle to attend the concert when that highfalutin concert pianist came to town. But it was a special occasion, and everyone they knew was going. So Charlie and Myrtle went too. And Myrtle decided right then and there that what she wanted more than life itself was to play the piano.

Charlie tried to talk her out of it. No one in Myrtle's family was any good at music. Couldn't carry a tune in a bucket, the lot of them. In fact, when her Uncle Teddy played the fiddle, he cleared out the whole house. Even the neighbors went to town to escape the sound. Besides, Charlie argued, they couldn't possibly afford a piano. And how would they get it out to the island? Where would they fit one inside their small lighthouse?

But Myrtle was as stubborn as her Uncle Teddy. If she couldn't find a dad-gum way, she'd make one! Before Charlie could count to ten she'd bought a cheap, used piano (that was always out of tune) and hauled it over to the island on her brother Jamie's fishing boat. She would have kept it at the foot of their bed if Charlie hadn't drawn the line there. So Myrtle put Charlie's favorite rocking chair and table out in the woodshed and installed her piano in the main living space.

From that day on, it was practice, practice, practice. Morning, noon, and night Myrtle sat at the piano with her songbook open, plunking away at the keys. At first, there was not much to hear, and Charlie could ignore the sour sounds. But after a few months, she got better . . . and a lot worse. There were parts of her song that sounded pretty good; but she never, ever got that one line right. *Dah-dah-dum-dum-*

PLAYIN' PIANO

BLAT, went the piano, every time. Twelve weeks in a row she'd been playing the same song without any improvement. Sometimes she'd continue after the first BLAT, and that was even worse. *Dum-dum-BLAT-BLAT-ding!*

There was nowhere on the small island that Charlie could go to get away from the sound, even when he sat in his favorite rocker out in the woodshed with cotton in his ears. Myrtle's new hobby was the source of much contention between husband and wife, who had never argued before. Now they argued every day.

"At least try to learn another song," Charlie begged his wife. But Myrtle was stubborn.

"I ain't going to learn another song until I've mastered this one. You've got to practice to get better, Charlie."

"Your Uncle Teddy practices his fiddle every Saturday night," Charlie snapped, "and he hasn't gotten any better in fifty years."

But Myrtle refused to listen. She just went back to her piano and started playing again. *Dah-dah-dum-dum-BLAT/ Dum-dum-BLAT-BLAT-ding.* Charlie went upstairs to polish the light. He put wax in his ears, but even that did not completely muffle the sound.

Things came to a head the day a nor'easter roared down on the island. Charlie and Myrtle were holed up together in the lighthouse hour after hour after hour. Charlie's chores were swiftly completed, and aside from regular checks on the light and a quick sweep of the beaches to make sure no ships were in danger, Charlie had nothing to do but sit and carve decoy ducks. And Myrtle played the piano. Hour after hour after hour. *Dah-dah-dum-dum-BLAT/Dum-dum-BLAT-BLAT-ding.*

Around 4 P.M. Charlie leapt to his feet and shouted at his wife to stop playing the blasted song. Myrtle leapt to her feet and shouted that she was going to practice until she got it right. After a brief but fierce argument, Myrtle sat down at the piano and started playing again. *Dah-dah-dum-dum-BLAT/ Dum-dum-BLAT-BLAT-ding.*

Then something in Charlie snapped.

A little while later, he felt bad about the way he chopped up the piano with his axe. After all, it was a valuable instrument. Try as he might, though, he couldn't feel bad about doing the same to Myrtle.

Charlie put on his oilskins, took up a shovel, and dug a grave out back of the woodshed. He buried all the little pieces of Myrtle with all the little pieces of her piano. He figured she would have wanted it that way. Later that night, with the nor'easter raging and pounding the island, and the lighthouse rattling and shaking wildly in the blast, Charlie got the best sleep he'd had in months. No more piano playing, ever.

The nor'easter blew itself out sometime the next morning. The island was peaceful and quiet once again, with no music at all save for the lap of the waves and the soughing of the wind through the pine trees. Charlie spent the rest of the day cleaning the blood off the floor and walls of the lighthouse. After that, he did his daily duties, moved his favorite rocking chair and table back into the main room, and carefully noted in the logbook the terrible tragedy that had befallen his wife during the storm.

Myrtle, according to the log, had been swept out to sea by a huge wave while heroically patrolling the beaches, helping Charlie look for shipwrecks.

In the middle of the night, Charlie was startled awake by a familiar sound. *Dah-dah-dum-dum-BLAT/Dum-dum-BLAT-BLAT-ding*. He sat bolt upright with an oath. It sounded just like Myrtle playing on the piano. But that was impossible—she was buried behind the woodshed!

Charlie leapt out of bed and felt around for his axe. *Blast!* He must have left it in the woodshed. He picked up a large piece of firewood and carefully stepped through the door into the main room, while the piano played its sour tune again and again. Charlie stared in astonishment at the glowing green translucent piano that stood once again in the place where Myrtle had put it. He could see his rocking chair and the end table right through the dad-blame instrument, which was somehow contriving to share space with them. The keys of the ghostly piano were playing all by themselves. *Dah-dah-dum-dum-BLAT/Dum-dum-BLAT-BLAT-ding*.

Then he heard Myrtle's voice coming from the stairway leading up to the light. "Charlie, over and over I told you . . . I ain't going to learn another song until I've mastered this one. You should have listened to me!"

Charlie whirled around and gazed toward the stairs. Standing a third of the way up the spiral staircase was the translucent white figure of his dead wife. And in her hands, she held his axe.

5

The Specter in the Graveyard

I sat at the bar, nursing my beer and watching as Eddie Johnson came through the door. He called general greetings to his friends as he weaved his way through the smoky room and sat down on the opposite side of the bar.

"What'll it be, Eddie?" asked Joseph, as if he didn't already know.

"Just a soda for me, Joe," Eddie said. Around some of the tables, men were nodding knowingly to each other. But Bart, who was visiting from the next village, stared at Eddie in disbelief. Eddie was known in three counties for his incredible drinking capacity.

"A soda?" Bart asked in shock. "Eddie, what happened to you? I never heard you order soda before!"

There was a familiar gleam in Eddie's eyes when he looked at the out-of-town chap. Eddie loved to tell folks the story of how he came to be sober. And everyone in town loved to hear it. Conversations all over the room came to an abrupt halt as Eddie moved down the bar to sit next to Bart.

"Well, Bart, I ain't had a drink in over three months," Eddie began. "My missus was after me to give up drinking. She always said the Devil would drag me right down to Hell if I didn't mend my ways. But I wouldn't listen to her. No sir, I was the first one in the bar and the last one out most every night."

"I remember," said Bart. "What happened?"

Everyone in the tavern leaned forward to listen as Eddie told his tale.

One dark, windy night last summer Eddie was walking home from the bar and got lost. He'd had a tad too much to drink and got himself turned around—couldn't figure out which way was home. The night was pitch-black, and Eddie couldn't see his hand in front of his face. Somehow, he made his way into the churchyard and found himself in the cemetery. He was sure he was in the cemetery on account of all the crosses and stones with fancy carvings on them.

Ah, ha! Eddie thought to himself. *I know how to get home now!*

As he walked through that cemetery, a strong breeze picked up and started howling around his head. He could hear creepy voices in that wind, moaning, "Eddie . . . Eddie . . ." Skin crawling and hands as cold as ice, Eddie started hurrying homeward as fast as he could, eager to leave the dark cemetery.

Suddenly, the ground opened up in front of him. Eddie stopped short, barely managing to keep his balance without falling into the hole. Then a skeletal hand reached up and wrapped itself around his leg. Eddie gave a shout and tried to break away, but the hand tripped him and pulled him down into the hole.

Eddie fell a long, long way. Finally, he landed on the bottom with a tremendous thump that knocked the breath

THE SPECTER IN THE GRAVEYARD

right out of him. The wind blew harder and harder, filling that deep hole with swirling air. Unearthly voices kept moaning his name: "Eddie . . . Eddie . . ." and the skeletal hand gripped his leg so hard he thought his bones would break. Eddie knew then that the Devil had come for him; come to take him down to Hell because of all his drinking, just like his wife had said.

Suddenly, the hand gripping his leg loosened up. It started to glow from the inside. Backing up against the wall, Eddie watched as the skeleton hand rose into the air. A robe formed around the skeleton hand and became a glowing specter of death that stared down at Eddie with fathomless, empty eyes. It had a ghastly skull that filled the hood.

"Eddie . . . Eddie . . ." the wind moaned as it leaked around the terrible figure before him. Then a voice came from the skull of the specter.

"You can't get out!" the specter intoned in the deep, intense tones of the dead. "You can't get out."

"God save me!" Eddie cried in fear.

Suddenly, he was filled with a miraculous strength that could have come only from heaven itself. Giving a great leap, Eddie reached for the top of the hole. The specter made a grab for his leg, but he avoided it and scrambled up to the top. The unearthly breeze tried to knock Eddie back into the hole, but he started singing "Glory Hallelujah," and his song cut right through those moaning voices. Then Eddie was free and running for home.

"And I haven't had a drink from that day to this," Eddie said, concluding his tale. "God saved me from the Devil and I ain't never going back. I've started going to church every

Sunday with me wife, and now she's the happiest woman in town. I've been given a second chance, Bart, and I don't mean to waste it."

Bart was pop-eyed with amazement. He was so impressed with the tale that he bought Eddie another soda and even drank one himself.

Now that the story was over, the other men in the bar started talking amongst themselves—all except old Tom Miller, who was sitting at a corner table, shaking with silent laughter. I was intrigued. I thought that Eddie's story was terrifying and inspiring, but not funny. Why was the old man laughing? I took my beer over and joined him at the table.

"Why are you laughing, Tom Miller?" I asked.

Tom let out a happy cackle. "Can't tell you, Fred. It's a secret," he said.

"Come on, Tom. You know I can keep a secret," I said.

I'd never told Tom's wife about the time he stole her ugly new apron to make a scarecrow. She still talked about the mystery whenever she came to visit with my wife.

Tom nodded. "Yep, I reckon you can." Then he told me another version of Eddie's tale.

Tom just happened to be taking the shortcut through the cemetery one dark and windy night last summer. And he fell right into a fresh-dug hole that was prepared for ol' Jeb Thompson's funeral the next day. It was a big, deep hole, and he couldn't get out, no matter how much he scrambled up the sides. The dirt kept crumbling under his hands. Tom figured he was stuck in there until morning. The mortician would be along pretty early, and he could fetch a ladder to get Tom out.

About an hour later, Tom was napping at the bottom of the hole when he awoke to the sound of some loud, off-key singing. It was Eddie Johnson walking home from the bar. Eddie must have been real drunk, because he was all turned around and kept trying to find his way home through the cemetery. Eddie's voice kept getting closer and closer. Tom yelled his name, hoping Eddie would help him out of the hole. But instead, Eddie fell into the grave, right on top of Tom.

Eddie scrambled around some and tried to climb out of the hole, just like Tom had. Finally, Tom said, "Eddie, you can't get out that way." And Eddie jumped straight up in the air. Tom had never seen anyone jump so high. Eddie did a little flip near the top of the hole, grabbed the edge, and was gone before Tom could say another word. Tom had been hoping they could boost each other out of the hole, but Eddie was already halfway home before Tom knew what had happened. So Tom had to wait until the mortician came in the morning to get out of the hole after all.

After the funeral, Tom heard Eddie telling some of his friends about the "specter in the graveyard." He was so sincere about quitting his drinking that Tom didn't have the heart to tell him the real story. "The mortician must have told Eddie's wife what really happened," Tom concluded, "because she baked me an apple pie and sent me a bouquet of her best roses to thank me!"

I laughed until the tears came to my eyes. Tom Miller swore me to secrecy, and I promised with a good will. Then I made my way out of the bar, pausing to thump Eddie on the shoulder and thank him for the fine example he was setting for the community. Eddie beamed at me and took another swig of soda.

"Thank you, Fred. I owe it all to God, who saved me from that terrible specter," he said piously.

What else could I say, but "Amen"?

6

The Lady in Red

We didn't believe in ghosts, so when the fellow checking us into the hotel warned us that our room on the sixth floor was haunted, we just laughed. There were a lot of crazy people out there who believed in ghosts and wanted to stay in a haunted hotel, but Marie and I weren't two of them. I'd chosen the Mizpah for our weekend getaway because I'd liked the description of the hotel and its amenities, not because it had a phantom.

Just for kicks, Marie asked the fellow who it was that supposedly haunted our room. He told us that it was a ghost called "The Lady in Red"—a prostitute who was strangled by a jealous boyfriend. Her tormented spirit still lingered in the hotel, and she was said to follow guests around and to play with the gaming equipment in the casino.

"A gambling ghost?" I laughed. The boy glared at me, and I felt sorry for making a joke about something he obviously believed in. We said a hasty goodnight and headed up to the sixth floor. After unpacking our bags, we went down to the casino to play a few games. I waved cheerfully to the young man at the desk and reported that we'd seen no ghosts—a comment that he did not deign to acknowledge.

Marie and I had a wonderful time playing the slot machines. We grabbed some dinner, then headed to the casino for a little more gambling before we turned in. I actually won fifty dollars, which amazed my pretty wife, who had never won anything in her life. Feeling full and happy, we quit the casino and walked arm and arm to the elevator.

"Do you think we'll see the Lady in Red?" I asked Marie as we entered the elevator. She pressed the button and then turned to give me a sarcastic smile.

"Of course. She'll waltz through the wall, right before our eyes," Marie said. I laughed and gave her a kiss. The elevator door opened too soon, and reluctantly I released my wife and escorted her down the hallway.

As we neared our room, Marie gasped and grabbed my arm. I stopped and looked at her. She pointed, wide-eyed, toward the far end of the hallway.

Before our eyes, the glowing figure of a woman came hurrying toward us. I shivered superstitiously, my skin prickling in the sudden cold as the Lady in Red rushed passed us and walked right through the wall next to our room.

"Good lord, there really is a ghost in our room!" I gasped. Beside me, Marie gave a tiny cry of sheer terror and started shaking like a leaf. I put both my arms around her, my eyes still glued to the wall where the ghost had vanished.

"I am not going into that room," Marie cried against my chest. "No way!" Her face was pale and her black eyes wide with fear.

I didn't much feel like going in there either, but we had gotten a special deal for two nights, paid in advance and

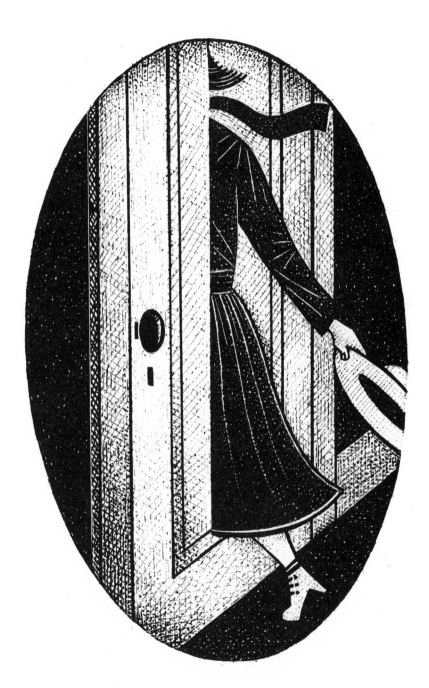

THE LADY IN RED

nonrefundable. I didn't want to waste our money. In the end, Marie stayed out in the hallway while I went to investigate the room. I wrenched open the door, turned on the light, and searched every corner for the Lady in Red. She was gone.

Even with my repeated reassurances, Marie refused to set foot in the haunted room. In the end, I had to go down to the desk and request a room on another floor. The boy didn't say much when I told him we had seen the Lady in Red, but he gave me a know-it-all smirk that made me want to smack him as he assigned us to a room on the ground floor.

Marie barely got a wink of sleep that night. She kept waking up, afraid that the Lady in Red would come walking through the wall and do terrible things to us. We were up at dawn and had checked out of the Mizpah by breakfast the next day. So much for our romantic weekend away!

From that day on, Marie made sure that she was the one who booked our hotels. She was careful to inquire about any ghosts that might haunt the premises before she made a reservation. One haunted hotel was enough for her.

7

When the samurai warrior Kane first came to California from Tokyo, he brought with him a new wife, the beautiful Ishi. She was an ideal wife: gentle, attentive, and obedient as well as a wonderful cook and homemaker. She always referred to Kane as "Husband" in the old style, which pleased him greatly. Kane was the envy of his new neighbors, and he and Ishi lived for several years in happiness.

But Kane was a proud man, the eldest child of indulgent parents, and he believed that nothing was too good for such a one as he. When a wealthy family of high rank moved into the neighborhood, Kane cast his eye upon their lovely daughter and desired her. The beauty and obedience of Ishi no longer pleased him. In his mind Ishi was second best, and Kane plotted to rid himself of his unwanted wife so he could woo and win the fair Aiko.

On the way home from a great banquet one stormy night, Kane pushed his young wife over the cliff into the bay. No one heard Ishi's scream through the howl of the wind and rain. No one suspected foul play when a distraught Kane came rushing back to the banquet hall, shouting for help because his poor wife had slipped in the mud and fallen over the edge of the cliff. The searchers found Ishi's broken body at dawn. Her long, black hair was tangled with seaweed, her beautiful face was crushed by the rocks on the beach, and her teeth were shattered.

Kane acted the part of the bereaved husband to perfection. He gave Ishi a splendid funeral. It wasn't until he was alone in his house after the neighbors had all gone away that Kane relaxed and drank to his success. In a month he would woo and wed the lovely Aiko, and her wealth would become his. Kane laid himself down upon his mat, rejoicing in the absence of Ishi and dreaming of his new love.

Outside, the wind whipped against the house, making the walls rattle and shake. A stray breeze swept through the sleeping-room with a sibilant whisper: "Vengeance. Vengeance." The breeze hissed and slapped the sleeping samurai. Kane rolled over restlessly as the door to the room slowly slid open. Moonlight streamed through the doorway, waking the warrior. Kane sat up and blinked as a hideously broken figure slowly stepped into the room. The wind whipped its long, seaweed-tangled black hair over the dirty, bloodstained kimono. Its face was crushed and broken, with one eyeball hanging by a thread from the socket. The ghost of Ishi reached out a bony hand toward her husband, smiling horribly through the shattered remains of her teeth. "Vengeance," she whispered, stretching her bloodstained hand caressingly toward Kane's face. "Vengeance."

Kane screamed in terror and tripped over the mat in his haste to flee from the dreadful figure. He leapt out of the window and ran to a neighbor's house, gibbering in fear. His

VENGEANCE

neighbors, mistaking his fear for overwhelming grief, welcomed him into their home and insisted he spend the rest of the night with them.

Kane tried to behave normally the next day, but as night fell his hands began to shake with fear, and he could not bring himself to enter his house. Instead, the samurai took his mat to an abandoned house in the neighborhood, determined to sleep within its ruins so that the ghost of Ishi could not find him. He left a paper lantern burning over his mat to keep away the shadows and finally fell into a dreamless sleep.

At the stroke of midnight, the wind began whipping against the abandoned house, whistling through the cracks and causing the ivy growing through a break in the wall to sway and grasp like bony, bloodstained hands. "Vengeance," the wind hissed. Kane woke with a start. Above him, the breeze tossed the lantern. The candle guttered, and the paper caught fire in several places. Slowly, two eyes burned themselves into the paper, and a wide grinning mouth with the shattered remains of teeth took shape. "Vengeance," the mouth whispered as the ivory hands reached out caressingly toward Kane. "Vengeance."

Kane grabbed his sword and hacked at the cloying, entangling vines. They were trying to strangle him, but he managed to free an arm and cut them away from his body. Above him, the face in the lantern laughed. "Vengeance," it cried. "I seek vengeance, Husband."

Kane broke free from the vines and fled from the abandoned house, followed by the sound of Ishi's laughter. He ran back to his neighbor's home and begged for shelter. Moved by the apparent grief of the samurai, they took him in and insisted he stay with them until the sharp edge of his sadness had blunted. This suited Kane well. While he stayed with his neighbors, the ghost of Ishi remained at bay.

A month passed. Kane continued to play the bereaved husband, and continued to sleep in his neighbor's house. But people began to notice that the grieving samurai would sometimes smile when in the company of Aiko. His friends and fellow warriors contrived to bring the two together as often as possible.

One day over tea, two of Kane's fellow samurai suggested that Kane marry Aiko. Hiding his triumphant grin in his cup, Kane haltingly asked them if they thought it would be proper, so soon after the passing of Ishi. Entirely proper, his friends assured him as a gust of wind slammed against the inn where they drank, causing the walls to rattle and shake. A stray breeze swept through the room with a sibilant whisper: "Vengeance. Vengeance." The breeze swirled through the steam rising from the teapot, shaping it into the broken form of a woman. The eyes of Kane's warrior friends glazed over. They both leapt to their feet, drawing their swords. Kane ducked and parried their blows, shouting: "What is wrong? Why are you attacking me?"

"Vengeance," hissed the rattling wind. "Vengeance," whispered the figure in the steam from the teapot, stretching its hand toward Kane's face. "Vengeance," chanted the two samurai together, their faces rigid, their bodies under the control of Ishi's ghost.

Kane upset the table, pouring hot tea over his friends. As he fled out the inn door, he heard swearing and gasping as the sting of the hot water pulled the warriors from their trance.

Kane did not pause until he reached a bend in the road. Only then did he look back. The giant, broken figure of Ishi towered over the inn, her crushed face and lolling eyeball leering at him mockingly. "Vengeance," she cried, stretching a hand caressingly toward him. Her bony arm grew longer and longer, until it reached the place where Kane was standing, transfixed.

At the last moment, Kane regained his senses and swung his sword at the hand, chopping it off. It fell to the ground at his feet and melted away. The towering ghost of Ishi laughed mockingly and vanished as Kane's friends came out the door of the inn. They remembered nothing of the ghost and were annoyed with their friend for spilling tea on them. Kane apologized many times before they would forgive him.

Shaken though he was by the reappearance of the ghost, Kane was still determined to woo and win the fair Aiko. He approached her father the next morning and was given permission to marry the daughter. Kane moved back to his home that afternoon and began preparing the house for his new bride. Then he grimly stayed awake all that night, expecting a visitation from the ghost. None came.

For a week Kane waited on edge for Ishi to appear, but her ghost had vanished. Relieved, Kane decided it was safe to bring Aiko and her family to see the home in which she would soon live. Proudly, he showed them each room in the house. Aiko was very much taken with the sleeping-room and lingered there while Kane took her parents out to the garden.

As he escorted Aiko's parents back into the house, he felt a hand on his arm, pulling him back into the garden. Kane turned and found himself face to face with a young, beautiful

Ishi, who kissed him and whispered a single word in his ear: "Vengeance." Laughing lightly, Ishi danced away, waving once toward the sleeping-room window. Still in shock from the encounter, Kane turned and saw Aiko silhouetted in the window, a look of bitter betrayal on her lovely face. Kane rushed indoors and tried to explain to his bride-to-be. The girl she had seen kiss him was a young cousin who was trying to make mischief, he told her. Aiko was placated, but from that time on did not trust Kane.

Fearing that Aiko might end the betrothal, Kane pressed forward with his suit, arranging for a grand engagement feast to prove his devotion to her. Friends, neighbors, and family came to the banquet hall and made merry over food and wine. Kane was pleased with the success of his feast. Aiko was smiling and warm, as she had not been since visiting his house. But when he looked up, he saw the beautiful young Ishi come into the room and stand demurely in the corner, facing him. Kane tried to distract Aiko so she would not notice Ishi, but Aiko was made suspicious by his sudden nervousness and she drew away from him.

Across the room, Ishi laughed softly and began to change, her beautiful body twisting and breaking before Kane's eyes, her face collapsing inward and bleeding, her black hair tangling with seaweed, her eyeball popping out of its socket.

"Vengeance," she whispered, reaching a hand toward Kane caressingly.

Kane shouted: "No! No! Leave here at once!"

Around him, Aiko, her parents, and their guests stared at Kane, puzzled by his behavior. None of them could see the ghost. Drawing his sword, Kane leapt over the table and attacked the ghost of Ishi, who laughed merrily and grew larger and larger before his eyes. Several of Kane's friends grabbed him and tried to wrestle the sword away, but he shook them all off. The ghost of Ishi drifted out the door and Kane followed her, shouting that she would haunt him no more. Ishi's ghost ran away from the banquet hall along the cliff path, the way she had once before walked with her husband. Kane ran after her, shouting and cursing. Suddenly, the ghost turned at the spot where Kane had pushed her over the cliff. She rose up and up, growing as tall as a tree, her face crushed and bloody, the eyeball swaying, and her shattered teeth gleaming in the moonlight.

"Vengeance!" she screamed, lunging at Kane. The samurai yelled in fear and dodged away from the ghost. His foot slipped on the loose earth at the edge of the cliff. He pin-wheeled his arms for a moment, trying to regain his balance, and then fell backward over the edge.

Kane's samurai friends found his broken body on the beach, and they buried him beside Ishi. That same night, a terrible storm beat against the house where Kane had brought his new bride from Tokyo. A lightning bolt hit the roof, and the house burned to the ground. The neighbors claimed they could hear a voice in the foul wind that blew that night, saying one word, over and over: "Vengeance."

8

The Lincoln Death Train

I'd been transferred to the Hudson Division of the New York Central system and was working the rails on the main line between New York and Albany. I was on the late shift, but that was okay with me, since I was a bit of a night owl. After six weeks of stomping the tracks and mending the rails, I was feeling right at home in my new job.

Then, just before midnight on a clear spring night in late April, we got a report of some brush on the track near our station. I was sent out immediately to clear it away before the next train came. I had nearly an hour before it was due to arrive, and so I didn't hurry as I walked along the rails. It was surprisingly pleasant and warm. Overhead, the clouds obscured the moon, but the light from my lantern made a cheerful glow in the gloomy night.

Suddenly, a chilly wind swept over the rails with a whoosh, like a gust just before a thunderstorm. It was so strong that it nearly knocked me over. I staggered backward, swearing and windmilling my arms to keep my balance. I almost dropped the lantern, but I managed to catch it just as it slipped out of my hand.

Shivering in the sudden cold, I squinted down the track

and saw a huge blanket of utter darkness rolling toward me. It blanked out the rails, the trees, the sky, everything.

"Good lord, what is that?" I gasped. I leapt away from the track and started to run back toward the station, but the darkness swept up and over me before I had moved a yard. The lantern in my hand was snuffed out instantly.

I stopped, unable to see more than a few paces around me. To my right, the rails began to gleam with a strange blue light. I staggered backward, my pulse pounding in fear and dread. What was going on?

Then a headlight pierced the thick darkness. A train was coming, though no train was scheduled for that time. The headlight gleamed blue-white in the strange black fog, and when the train appeared, the rails brightened in response. A huge steam engine draped in black crepe approached, stacks bellowing forth a steady stream of smoke. The brass on the engine gleamed, and it pulled several flatcars along behind it. I stared into the windows of the engine but couldn't see any crew.

Just at the edge of hearing came the faint sound of music. I turned to look at the flatcars behind the engine, then gasped and backed up so far that I bumped into the trunk of a tree growing near the tracks. There on the train was a glowing orchestra of skeletons seated in a semicircle. They were playing a nearly soundless funeral dirge on glimmering black instruments. A violinist played passionately; a skeleton lifted a flute to its lipless mouth; a lone drummer sat waiting patiently for his cue from the skeletal conductor.

Then the orchestra was gone, and another glowing headlight pierced the blackness. I was trying unsuccessfully to push

THE LINCOLN DEATH TRAIN

my body through the bark and into the tree by this time. Another black train was approaching. A funeral train, I thought. Again, there was no one manning the engine, which pulled a single flatcar containing a black crepe–draped coffin. Swirling in the air around the train were the ghostly figures of soldiers dressed in the blue uniforms worn by the North during the Civil War. They lined up before my eyes, saluting the solitary coffin as it passed. Some of the ghosts staggered under the weight of their own coffins; some limped on one leg or sat in a wheeled chair, legless. Their eyes were fixed on the flatcar and the black-creped coffin. Then these phantoms were joined by soldiers from the Southern army, and all those lads saluted too, honoring the one who had fallen.

That's when I knew what I was seeing. This was the funeral train of Abraham Lincoln. I straightened up and saluted myself, having done my bit for the North many years ago.

The steam train moved slowly away, and with it went the darkness and the chill and the clouds that had obscured the moon. In my hand, the lantern sprang back to life. I blinked a few times and brushed away a tear. As the world around me brightened, I saw the reported brush littering the tracks right in front of me. Mechanically, I cleared it away and made sure the track was safe for the next train. Then I went back to the station.

The next morning, all the clocks on the Hudson Division were six minutes behind, and all the trains were running six minutes late. When I asked the stationmaster about it, he shook his head and told me not to worry. It was caused by the Lincoln Death Train, he said, which had stopped time as it ran by in the night.

9

Never Mind Them Watermelons

Well now, old Sam Gibb, he didn't believe in ghosts. Not one bit. Everyone in town knew the old log cabin back in the woods was haunted, but Sam Gibb just laughed whenever folks talked about it. Finally, the blacksmith dared Sam Gibb to spend the night there. If he stayed until dawn, the blacksmith said, he would buy him a whole cartload of watermelons. Sam was delighted. Watermelon was Sam's absolute favorite food. He ate so many of them that folks hereabouts said he had watermelon juice running in his veins instead of blood.

So Sam accepted the dare at once. He packed up his frying pan, sausages, matches, and pipe, and went right over to the log cabin to spend the night. There was only one room with a rough fireplace and a few rickety chairs, but Sam quickly made himself at home. He built a fire and settled down in a chair to enjoy his pipe.

When it drew near midnight, Sam decided it was time to cook up his dinner. He set the frying pan on the fire, placed the sausages in the pan, and then settled back into his chair for another smoke. Soon the small cabin filled with the delicious smell of frying meat. Sam crossed his legs and sank deeper into his seat with a happy sigh, thinking about all the watermelons he would be eating once he won this bet. He pulled out a copy of yesterday's newspaper and read it with enjoyment while his dinner sizzled and spat in the hearth.

As Sam was reading, he heard a creaking sound, and something stirred in the shadows. Looking up, he saw that a gnarled little creature with glowing red eyes had scurried out onto the hearth. It had a long forked tail, two horns on its head, claws at the ends of its hands, and sharp teeth that poked right through its large lips. The tiny imp spat right across the frying pan into the back of the fire. Sam frowned. *Now that wasn't nice*, he mused, *messing with another man's meat.*

The imp looked up at Sam with its glowing red eyes.

"There ain't nobody here tonight except you and me," the creature said. It had a voice like the hiss of flames. Sam's heart nearly stopped with fright, but he wasn't about to give up a pan full of fine sausages and a whole wagonload of watermelons without a fight.

Feigning indifference, Sam turned his whole attention to the meat sizzling in the frying pan. Leaning forward, he stirred the sausages. They looked all right and still smelled delicious, but he wasn't sure he wanted to eat something the imp had almost spat upon.

The imp was not pleased. It spat into the fire again, right next to the frying pan. Sam sat up with a jerk, heart pounding. He was equal parts scared and furious, but the fury won out. He had been looking forward to his meal all evening, and now this pesky devil had almost ruined it. Sam swatted at the imp, shouting, "Don't you spit in my meat!"

Quick as lightening, the imp kicked over the frying pan, spilling the meat into the fire. Then it lunged up at Sam, clawing him between the eyes. Sam reeled back in pain as the imp returned to its place on the hearth. There was a moment of heavy silence. Sam clutched his bleeding forehead and stared numbly at the imp. Then the creature turned its red eyes on Sam and said again, "There ain't nobody here tonight except you and me."

Sam stared, mesmerized, into the imp's eyes. He felt as if he were falling into the very pit of hell. Sam began trembling from head to toe. He jumped to his feet, still clutching his bleeding forehead. Even a cartload of watermelons wasn't worth this!

"There ain't gonna be nobody here but you in a minute," Sam Gibb told the gnarled creature.

Sam leapt straight for the nearest exit—which happened to be the window—and hightailed it down the lane, lickety-split. He ran so fast he overtook two rabbits being chased by a coyote. But it wasn't long before he heard the pounding of little hooves, and the gnarled creature with the red eyes caught up with him.

"You're making pretty good speed for an old man," said the creature to old Sam Gibb.

"Oh, I can run much faster than this," Sam Gibb said. He took off like a bolt of lightning, leaving the gnarled creature in the dust. As he ran past the blacksmith shop, the smithy came flying out of the forge to see what was wrong.

NEVER MIND THEM WATERMELONS

"Never mind about them watermelons," Sam Gibb shouted to the blacksmith without breaking his stride.

Old Sam Gibb ran all the way home and hid under his bed for the rest of the night. After that, he was a firm believer in ghosts and spooky creatures, and he refused to go anywhere near the old cabin in the woods.

10

Screaming Jenny

The old storage sheds along the tracks were abandoned shortly after the Baltimore & Ohio Railroad was built, and it wasn't long before the poor folk of the area moved in. The sheds provided shelter—of a sort—although the winter wind still pierced every crevice, and the rough fireplaces folks built within the poorly constructed sheds did little to keep the cold at bay.

My father had lost his job that fall, due to ill health that had forced him to stay too many days away from work. Mama took a job washing dishes and cleaning rooms at one of the local inns, but the money didn't stretch far in a family of six. We were turned out of our lodgings when our money ran short, and I don't know how we would have survived if one of my street friends hadn't told me about the abandoned storage units. I was the eldest son and earned as much money as I could hawking newspapers and running errands for some of the local merchants. Mama didn't like me leaving school so soon, but I was old enough to know my own mind, and we needed the money. Fortunately, between Mama and me, we made just enough to keep food on the table, so my little brother and two sisters were able to stay in school.

I looked over the abandoned storage shed, found it creaky but adequate, and moved the family in. We put Father and Mother's bed next to the rusty wood stove I'd purchased for a song at a debtor's auction, where Father had the best chance of recovering his health. We put the children's beds in the opposite corner and divided the room with a blanket hung from a rope during the night. My little brother and I shared one bed, and my two sisters shared another.

It wasn't long after we moved in that I met a gentle, kindly woman named Jenny. She was pushing fifty and had a sweet, weathered face that was worn with care, and dark brown hair that was streaked with silver. I took to her at once, which was unusual for me, for I was a solemn, introspective lad.

Jenny lived alone in one of the smaller sheds, having fallen on hard times. She had no family to protect her, and she was forced to do odd jobs to survive. She could no longer afford to rent a room, so she moved into one of the storage sheds when it became available.

Jenny never had enough to eat, and in the cold winter months, her tiny fire barely put out enough heat to keep her alive. Still, she kept her spirits up and was the first one at the door whenever one of the "shed families" had trouble. She often came to play checkers with my invalid father while Mama was at work, and he came to look upon her as a second mother. My sisters and my little brother adored her. They brought home little crafts from their school to give her, and they often did their homework in her shed. I learned from some of the people in our impromptu village that Jenny always tried to help other folks when they took sick or needed food, sometimes going without herself so that another could eat.

One cold evening in late autumn, Jenny sat shivering over her fire while my little brother perched in the corner doing his homework. When I looked in on them, I saw Jenny drinking broth out of a wooden bowl. And then, to my horror, I realized that Jenny's dress was on fire. A spark had flown from the small stove and lit the hem of her skirt. Intent on filling her aching stomach, Jenny did not notice her flaming clothes until the fire had burnt through the heavy wool of her skirt.

I gave a yell of alarm, and she startled in surprise, nearly dropping her bowl. "Jenny, you're on fire!" I shouted, glancing around for a bucket of water or a blanket. There was nothing available to douse the blaze.

Leaping up in terror, Jenny threw her broth over the licking flames, but the fluid did nothing to help.

"Drop on the ground and roll," I shouted, running to her and trying to push her to the floor. In her terror, Jenny did not heed me. Instead, she broke away and ran outside. She made for the train tracks, screaming for help. I started to follow her, but my little brother gave a shout of dismay, pointing at my trousers, and I realized that I too had caught fire when I'd tried to help Jenny. I flung myself on the floor of the shed, rolling around to put out the fire, while my brother cried hysterically and pummeled me with his shirttail.

As soon as we'd smothered the fire in my trousers, I leapt up to follow Jenny, telling my brother to run home and get help. In the distance, I could see her still running along the tracks, flames engulfing her body. I raced after her, shouting desperately for her to drop on the ground and roll, just as I had done.

SCREAMING JENNY

Jenny was making for the Harper's Ferry train station, which was only a short distance from the shed village. She probably thought they had enough water there to douse the flames. But the station was still too far away, and the wind she was kicking up by running had turned the licking flames into a glowing inferno that engulfed her from head to toe.

As I limped desperately toward the tracks, Jenny's screams grew more horrible. The pain was blinding her to everything else, and her steps were slowing down. I thought I might be able to reach her, but just then I heard a train whistle. I whirled to gaze up the tracks and then shouted desperately and ran toward Jenny. She had staggered blindly onto the rails just west of the station, a ball of fire that barely looked human. In her agony, she had not seen the glowing headlight of the train rounding the curve or heard the screech of the brakes as the engineer spotted her fire-eaten figure and tried to stop. I was still twenty yards away when her terrible screams broke off as the train mowed her down.

Alerted by the whistle, the crew from the station came running as the engineer halted the train and ran back down the tracks toward poor Jenny, whose body was still burning. I reached her at the same time as the engineer, who shouted to the stationmaster to bring water. But both of us knew it was already too late. Jenny was dead. The men doused the fire and carried her body back to the train station, while I limped home to comfort my little brother and tell my parents the terrible news.

Jenny was given a pauper's funeral, which was attended by everyone in the shed village. She had no money for a tombstone and was buried in an unmarked grave in the local church-yard. Within a few days, another poverty-stricken family had moved into her shack, and Jenny was forgotten by almost everyone. Everyone except for me and my family, who had loved her like a grandmother.

I had nightmares every night for six months, seeing my beloved friend burning over and over. I kept reliving the scene, trying to figure out what I might have done differently to save Jenny. My parents reassured me again and again that I had done everything possible. Jenny had died because she panicked, plain and simple. It took a long time for me to believe what my folks had said, but when I finally did, the nightmares ceased.

A year to the day after Jenny's death, I was coming home late from one of my odd jobs when I heard the sound of a train approaching the bend near our shed. I glanced toward the tracks and stopped dead, staring, as a glowing ball appeared in the distance. It hurled itself toward the bend, gradually assuming the shape of a burning woman running for the train station. It was Jenny. I could hear her screaming as the train whipped around the corner. Too late to stop, the engineer plowed over the glowing figure before he could bring the train to a screeching halt. I watched in horror as the glowing figure lay broken and burning for a moment on the tracks. Then it disappeared.

Leaping from the engine, the engineer ran back down the tracks to search for a mangled, burning body, but there was no one there. I wanted to tell him that he had run over a ghost, but I was afraid he would think I was crazy. I heard later that the shaken engineer brought his train into the station and reported the incident to the stationmaster. After hearing his tale, the stationmaster remembered poor, dead Jenny and realized that her ghost had returned to haunt the tracks where she had died.

I went home on legs that would barely hold me up and told Mama the whole story. She listened with a white face and grimly pursed lips. That night I heard her talking softly with Father. The next day, my parents told us that we were moving into lodgings in town. Mama had saved up enough to put down a deposit on the place, and Father was well enough to work part-time in the mercantile. We packed up our things and left the storage shed behind forever.

The town was soon awash with stories about the ghost of "Screaming Jenny." She was seen several more times, much to the horror of the B&O engineers, who rounded the curve just west of the station and found themselves face to face with the burning phantom. I always had nightmares after hearing of another appearance of Screaming Jenny, and my parents decided it would be best if the family moved to another town to get away from the horrible memories that the ghost evoked.

I never saw the phantom again, though I later heard that the ghost of Screaming Jenny appeared on the tracks every year on the anniversary of her death, once more making her deadly run toward the Harper's Ferry station.

11

Piece by Piece

There once was a crazy ghost over in Poughkeepsie that got folks so plumb scared that nobody would stay more than one night in its house. It was a nice old place—or had been, that is, until the ghost began making its presence known. The owners got so riled up that they finally packed up one morning and moved away.

The house agents sold the place a couple of times, but none of the new owners would stay once the ghost made an appearance. After a few years of this, the place was abandoned. No one in their right mind would go near the house—not even kids on a dare, and you know what they are like.

Now when my friend Joe heard that a fancy old house in Poughkeepsie was selling for dirt cheap, he decided to go have a look. He asked me about it and I told him about the spook, describing its purported antics in gruesome detail. Joe just laughed at me. "I don't believe in ghosts," he said and went to visit the agent selling the house.

Well, the agent gave Joe a key, but refused to look at the old house with him, which should have told Joe something. But Joe's a stubborn man who won't listen to reason. He even waited until after dark to visit the house for the first time, just to drive home his point.

Joe got to the house around 9 P.M. The property had fallen into considerable disarray, and the house looked like it should indeed be haunted. The garden was overgrown, and Joe had to weave his way between briar bushes and overgrown hedges just to get to the porch. The porch sagged in places, and the front steps moaned menacingly when he climbed them.

I was lurking outside one of the windows so I could watch what happened without participating in the action. I grinned a little at the sight of my foolish friend fighting to get the warped front door to open when he turned the large, fancy key the realtor had given him. Joe tugged and cursed and pushed with his shoulder until the door suddenly slammed open, spilling him onto the dusty floor of the entranceway. *That should have alerted the ghost*, I thought, smudging off the glass before me with my fist to get a better view inside.

Joe climbed to his feet, brushed the dirt off his clothes, and looked around in the light of the gas lantern he carried. It was a large entrance hall, well-proportioned but neglected, with cobwebs and dust everywhere. As Joe paused near the door to get his bearings, he heard a thump from the top of the staircase facing him. He jumped and looked up as a disembodied voice began to moan, starting down low and then rising until it shrieked higher than a soprano singing Wagner.

A glowing leg appeared out of nowhere and rolled down the steps, landing right next to Joe's feet. Joe gasped and stood frozen to the spot as the leg flopped around a few times, trying to walk all by itself. Then an arm appeared and rolled down to meet the leg. The long fingers stretched out and grabbed Joe's shoe. Joe kicked at it with his free foot until it relaxed its

PIECE BY PIECE

grip. Next came a foot, which thudded slowly down the steps, one at a time, with a hollow bumping like a drum of doom. Another arm rolled after it, and then a torso.

Glowing body parts kept popping into existence and plummeting down the steps toward Joe. They were bumping and jostling each other, and the glowing pieces were starting to look less and less like a loose pile and more and more like a gruesome, blood-stained, headless body.

Joe held his ground a lot longer than anyone else ever had, but when a screaming head appeared at the top of the steps and started rolling down toward him, Joe had had enough. With a shriek that could wake the dead—those that weren't already up and haunting the house, that is—Joe ran for his life, out of the house, out of the street, and right out of town, leaving his car behind him. I made a hasty exit myself when the head looked up from its place on top of the blood-stained body and winked at me through the window.

Joe called me the next day and asked me to drive his car down to the hotel where he had spent the night. He was headed back to Manhattan and refused to come within 50 miles of Poughkeepsie ever again.

The agent gave up trying to sell the place after that, and the house fell into ruin and was eventually torn down.

12

Dismal Swamp

Jared couldn't believe it when his fiancée Bethany fell ill just a few short weeks before their marriage. She was a strong, healthy girl—the daughter of his neighbor—but she just faded away before his eyes. He tried everything he could to save her, contacting the local physician and even riding his horse many weary miles to get a specialist from the city. But nothing could be done. The pain radiated out from her middle so intensely that the local doctor decided to keep her on morphine at all times.

There came a day when Jared refused to leave Bethany's side, knowing that at any moment she could go. He slept in a chair during the night and sat on the side of her bed during the day. She was so heavily drugged that she didn't recognize him until her final moments. The morning before they were to have wed, she called his name, and her eyes cleared for the first time since she fell ill. Jared took her into his arms and they spoke quietly of the life they would have together "someday." He held her long after she gasped out her last breath.

Jared was inconsolable. Long after Bethany's body lay buried beside the Dismal Swamp, he sat alone in his room, grieving for his lost love. He scorned food and sleep, depriving himself until his mind gave way under the strain. One morning,

DISMAL SWAMP

he came out into the kitchen as happy as he had been before Bethany's tragic illness. His mother was delighted at first, until something in his conversation revealed that he had lost touch with reality and thought that his betrothed was still alive. Jared now believed that Bethany had gone away for awhile because of a tiff with her parents, but he was sure that he could mend the rift between them.

"I will find her and apologize for them. Then she'll come home with me and we'll be married," he told his mother earnestly. "I will find her, Mama."

His family tried to reason with him, but Jared's mind was made up. His Bethany was missing, not dead, and he would listen to no one who suggested otherwise. He spent the majority of every day walking up and down the highways and byways, calling her name. After about a week, he became obsessed with the notion that she was living somewhere in the swamp, perhaps in one of the abandoned fishing shacks. She would never wish to be far from her parents, in spite of the breach he imagined between them.

"I will find her," he told his anxious family, passionate in his conviction. "I will find her and bring her home."

Something in his mother's expression worried him. He stepped forward and took her hand. "She is ill, Mama, and tired. I think she is afraid she is going to die."

His mother brightened a little with hope. This was the first time Jared had acknowledged that something more than an argument might have sent his Bethany from him.

"Don't worry," Jared continued. "I will hide her away from Death, so that he will never find her when he comes."

His eyes blazed with an insane fire that repelled his family. His mother tore her hands from his and turned away from the madness she could no longer deny. She covered her face with her hands, her body tense with pain.

Jared's father tried once again to convince him that his beloved lay dead beside the swamp, but Jared would not listen. He broke away from his father violently and ran off to the Dismal Swamp. Jared wandered about for days, living on roots and berries and sleeping at night in the dank marshland. Endlessly, he called out to his beloved to come to him, but there was no answer.

One evening at dusk, Jared stumbled upon Drummond's Pond, a 5-mile expanse of water in the middle of the Dismal Swamp. On the black surface of the water, he saw the soft blinking of fireflies dancing hither and thither across the black surface.

To his dazed eyes, the soft lights framed a beloved figure that beckoned to him wistfully and called out his name.

"Bethany, my love!" he exclaimed, overjoyed. "I see her life-light!"

To his maddened mind, it seemed that Bethany hovered over the waters—her spirit caught between this world and the next. A gesture either way would determine whether she lived or died. He saw her life-candle flickering behind her, growing more erratic and burning down toward nothing. If he didn't reach her in time, the candle would burn out, and she would be lost to him forever.

Jared, who could not swim, rushed around, frantically constructing a raft of cypress branches so that he could reach his love before she disappeared. Lashing the branches together with vines, he leapt on top of the flimsy craft and floated out to join the girl he had lost. As he drew near the center of the pond, a wind sprang up, and the raft was tossed and tumbled in the sudden waves. With a cry of alarm, Jared fell from the raft and sank down into the murky waters. He thrashed about desperately, his eyes on the fireflies dancing above the water, just out of reach.

"Bethany!" he screamed, the name choking off as water filled his mouth. "Beth . . . " the last bit was lost as his head went under for the final time.

The next day, Jared's drowned body was found by his father, who had come searching for his insane child. The family buried him next to Bethany.

Occasionally, visitors to Drummond's Pond still hear Jared's voice echoing dismally across the still waters as he searches for his beloved. And some brave souls who remain in the vicinity after dark claim that the phantoms of Jared and Bethany, reunited in death, sometimes float across the pond on a raft made of cypress branches, carrying a firefly lantern to light their way.

13

The Music Lesson

She had not been studying organ long, but already she loved it passionately and was contemplating a musical career when she finished school. There was only one thing that marred her enjoyment, and that was the lonely, nighttime practice sessions in the echoing, empty chapel. Something about the place frightened her. She never felt safe until she was actually in the organ loft.

Packing up her organ books, the girl left her dorm room and hurried down toward the arched cloisters that connected the school to the chapel. Already her skin was prickling, and goosebumps were rising on her arms as she thought of the empty church. *Don't be ridiculous,* she told herself, lifting her chin and straightening her shoulders.

The girl marched bravely into the lonely, echoing church. Its huge stained-glass windows loomed dark and bleak in the twilight, and she could hear every footstep ringing through the sanctuary as she walked. It was so very large and so very empty. Anything might be hidden in the dark shadows that lurked in each corner. She quickened her pace.

The girl began to relax when she reached the spiral stair-case leading up to the organ, and she gave a sigh of relief when she parted the velvet curtain at the top of the staircase and stepped into the loft. She put her books down and arranged herself on the bench, shivering a little in the sudden cold that swept around her. It was strange to feel such a chilly breeze on a warm night in early summer, she thought, feeling spooked.

The girl was about to put her feet on the pedals when suddenly a single pure note came from the organ. She froze in place and stared wide-eyed at the keyboard, which had just played all by itself. The chill around her increased perceptibly. Shudders of cold and fear shook her from head to toe. In that moment, she was convinced that she was not alone in the echoing darkness of the empty church.

A sudden movement by the velvet curtain caught her eye, and the girl turned her head. Standing in front of the curtain was a portly, middle-aged woman in a long, light-blue dress. The woman was flickering slightly in and out of existence like a bad filmstrip, and she was translucent. The girl could see the velvet curtain right through the phantom's body. The woman seemed to be staring at something . . . or someone . . . sitting on the bench with the girl.

Chills went up the girl's spine as she remembered the strange note that had come unaided from the organ. Convinced that she was occupying the same space as a ghostly organ student about to have a music lesson, the girl leapt to her feet and fled for the spiral staircase, even though that meant heading straight toward the other phantom. Head down, eyes on the floor, the girl ran right through the flickering woman blocking the velvet curtain. For a moment she was

THE MUSIC LESSON

eclipsed by a terrible cold that made her limbs shake and her stomach do flip-flops of sheer terror.

Then she was racing down the staircase, across the echoing aisles of the chapel and out the cloistered archways toward safety and the school. She told the whole story to her housemistress, even drawing her a picture of the flickering phantom, who was quickly identified as one of the founders of the school. The girl absolutely refused to go back to fetch her organ music, which was left in the loft until the next morning. And she never played the organ again.

14

Turnabout Is Fair Play

Old Uncle Phil was a tall scarecrow of a fellow who was jumpier than a grasshopper. He lived and worked on a small farm near Branchville, and he believed that the hostile world was largely populated with monsters and ghosts and spooks and witches and werewolves. Uncle Phil believed in just about every sort of scary critter that you can imagine. He shied away from shadows, jumped whenever anyone spoke to him, and lived in perpetual fear that someone, somewhere was out to get him.

Uncle Phil wore so many amulets that he chimed and rattled and clanked whenever he moved. Early in life, he took a trip to Pennsylvania Dutch Country to learn what the most powerful hex signs were so he could paint them on his house and barn. He even planted a special garden around his house that was full of trees and bushes and plants designed to thwart the forces of evil.

Uncle Phil hated to go outside after dark. He always carried a lantern with him so as not to be caught anywhere without light. He even took the long way home rather than walk through the "ominous" woods surrounding the river. He became so paranoid that he refused to shake hands with anyone because it might allow an evil spirit to enter him, and he never entered a house that had a cat, because he thought that the animal might be an imp or a witch's familiar.

Naturally, this attitude made Uncle Phil the butt of many jokes. Children in particular took a rather cruel delight in plaguing the old man. At first it was just small things, like stealing the apples from his orchard, tossing rocks into his path from behind trees, or tapping his shoulder when he was buying groceries in the store. The youngsters would howl with laughter when Uncle Phil yelped and whirled around, and they giggled and whispered whenever he complained about the goblins who stole all his apples away.

One summer a new family moved to town with two sons who were very naughty indeed. As soon as they learned about jumpy Uncle Phil, those boys became obsessed with tormenting him. They snuck out to his place one night and painted over all his hex signs. When Uncle Phil woke up the next morning, the barn and the house were bare. He ran all the way to town on foot—forgetting that he owned a horse—because he was sure the Devil had removed the hex signs in order to steal his soul away while he slept. The old man crouched in a pew in the local church and wouldn't leave until the minister had prayed over his house and the neighborhood painter had re-created the hex signs.

A week after this event, the boys gathered all of the black cats in town and put them into Uncle Phil's house while he was away. When Uncle Phil opened the door, his dog rushed into the front room; fur started flying everywhere as the black cats hissed and scratched and yowled and bit. Back ran Uncle Phil to the church, and back came the minister with some helpers to clear the house of black cats and bless it against any evil witches who wanted to curse Uncle Phil.

The boys were forced to lay low for a while after this incident, which had upset all the adults in town. The schoolchildren were subjected to a lecture on cruelty and instructed to report any mischief committed against Uncle Phil. Of course all the children knew who the culprits were, but no one told.

For a month Uncle Phil was left in peace. No fruit disappeared from his orchards, no mysterious ghost tapped his shoulder, no goblins tossed rocks at him from the trees. Then the boys came up with another plan. One night, they snuck in Uncle Phil's house through the parlor window, dragging a scarecrow inside with them. They set up the scarecrow so that it loomed over the poor sleeping man with one arm outthrust, as if it wanted to shake hands with him. Then they positioned a lantern on a tree branch just outside the second-story room so that the light illuminated the scarecrow's grotesque face. Once everything was in place, the boys started moaning and groaning and calling Uncle Phil's name from the yard outside his bedroom window.

Uncle Phil woke with a gasp and then screamed in sheer terror when his eyes encountered the scarecrow. Leaping off the bed, he dove out of his bedroom window and climbed to the very top of the tree. From his high perch Uncle Phil clutched desperately at the various charms he wore under his nightshirt and said the Twenty-third Psalm aloud. Below him the lantern rocked dangerously and then fell to the ground, setting fire to the woodpile beside the house. The boys stopped laughing when they realized that Uncle Phil's

TURNABOUT IS FAIR PLAY

house was on fire. They ran to the barn and wet some old sacks in the water barrel. Together, they managed to put out the fire, but not before the whole side of the house was scorched. In the tree above them, they could hear Uncle Phil begging God to spare him from the terrible devil who had come with his grotesque face and his flames to take Uncle Phil's soul.

Afraid of what their parents would do if they discovered the trick, the boys snuck into the house and removed the scarecrow before hightailing it home. In the morning Uncle Phil came down from the top of the tree and went to fetch the preacher. The minister and many of the leading citizens in town were amazed when they saw the huge scorch mark on the side of Uncle Phil's house where—he claimed—the Devil had come and tried to take away his soul.

Uncle Phil shivered and shook all morning as people came to inspect his house. He was still dressed in his nightshirt because he refused to go back inside to change. Finally, the minister's wife took Uncle Phil home with her and tucked him into bed with a bowl of hot soup. The minister had to perform a third ritual cleansing of the farm before Uncle Phil would return to his property.

The boys were afraid to play any more pranks after their last escapade ended so dramatically. Life went back to normal for Uncle Phil—at least, as normal as it could be for someone who believed in ghosts and goblins and witches and werewolves and all sorts of crazy critters. Then, about a month after the "Devil's visit," Uncle Phil passed away in his sleep. The whole town turned out for his funeral, and many folks were saddened that such a colorful figure had left their lives.

The boys felt terrible about the old man's death, afraid that their trick with the scarecrow might have weakened him and caused his final passing. But they were scared to confess that they were the ones who had played the trick on Uncle Phil. They grew very quiet in school and did their chores listlessly at home. Their mother was so worried by their lack of spirit that she started treating them with cod-liver oil and mustard plasters.

Nothing helped.

Two weeks after Uncle Phil's death, the boys woke to find their bedroom full of black cats. The boys shouted in alarm, which made the cats hiss and scratch and yowl and bite. Their parents came running into the room and were furious at the scene. The boys could not convince them that they did not know how the cats got there.

A week passed. When the boys came home from school one afternoon, they saw that a hex sign had been painted on their barn—the very same sign that they had painted over on Uncle Phil's barn. The boys yelled in terror and ran inside their house, pulling their mother away from her bread dough to look at the barn. But when they reached the far wall, the hex sign was gone.

For the next several days, the boys were tormented by an unseen foe. Rotten fruit would pelt them as they walked through the woods. Someone would tap their shoulders in the schoolyard, causing them to yelp and whirl around, only to find that no one was there. After dark the boys would hear the chiming and clanking sound of amulets as they walked along the shadowy lanes near their home.

One night, the boys woke to hear a voice moaning their names over and over again. They sat up in their beds and lit the lantern, which illuminated a grotesque scarecrow looming in the center of the room. The boys screamed in terror, and the younger lad leapt into bed with his brother as the scarecrow started to move toward them. "I have come for your soul," it moaned, waving its arms about.

Then the scarecrow started laughing. It shook a finger at the cowering boys, and they heard the chiming and clanking of amulets. One arm reached up and snatched off the scarecrow's head, revealing the glowing, partially transparent face of Uncle Phil.

"Gotcha!" said the ghost of Uncle Phil with a huge grin. Then he disappeared.

The boys were torn between abject terror and amusement. They clung together, alternating between laughing and crying until their parents came in to see what was causing all the ruckus. The teary-eyed boys told their parents the whole story, starting with the tricks they had played on Uncle Phil and ending with the pranks his ghost had pulled on them. They pointed out the wisps of hay on the floor and the painted sack that the ghost had used as a scarecrow's head.

When the boys finished their story, their father sat back against the wall and started to laugh heartily. "It serves you right," he said. "After all, turnabout is fair play!"

The boys had to agree with him. After that they stuck to their games and school rivalries and never played another practical joke again.

15

Don't Sell My House

When Tilly's daughter, Lisa, married a nice widower after an extremely short courtship, the newlyweds bought a beautiful new RV and had it installed on their property so Tilly could have a place of her own to live. It was a nice arrangement for her. She had her privacy, but she was close enough to walk to her daughter's house whenever she chose—which was often, because she and Lisa were very close.

Mark had built the house for his first wife, who had died of cancer two years before his marriage to Lisa. It was a small, two-story cottage with a finished basement. Tilly had her own key to the basement door so she could do her laundry whenever she pleased without disturbing her daughter and son-in-law.

About a year after Lisa and Mark's wedding, they found out that they were expecting twins. Tilly was delighted with the news that she was going to be a grandmother, but she was concerned that the house was rather small for a double addition to the family. After talking it over, Mark and Lisa put the cottage up for sale and started searching for a bigger house with enough property to house Tilly's RV. And that's when the problems began.

Tilly noticed it first. Suddenly, the cottage was filled from night until morning with the distinctive smell of expensive perfume. Lisa was allergic to perfume and never wore it, so the source of the smell was a mystery. The first time Mark smelled it, he turned pale and grimly told Tilly that it was the scent his dead wife had favored.

Then furniture that Lisa had rearranged when she first came to the little cottage abruptly moved back to its original place. Tilly knocked her shins several times on a side table that would not stay put. Dishes moved from one cupboard to another, the sofa was pushed back against the wall, and the books in Mark's study were taken out of their categories and put in alphabetical order, the way his former wife had kept them arranged. Tilly was sure that the ghost of Mark's first wife had returned to the little cottage. But why? If she was jealous of Lisa, why had it taken her a whole year to manifest herself?

One afternoon, Tilly was down in the basement doing her laundry while Mark and Lisa were out discussing the sale of the cottage with their attorney. They had just received a generous bid on the house and had decided to accept it. Tilly was emptying the washing machine when she became aware of movement by the staircase leading to the kitchen. Tilly turned and saw a young woman floating a foot above the staircase, wearing a white dress sprinkled with pink flowers. Tilly froze in shock, the laundry basket shaking in her hands.

"Don't sell my house," the young woman said.

Tilly swallowed convulsively, not sure what she should say or do.

"This is my house. Don't sell my house!" the woman said again. Her pretty face was suddenly transformed with rage, and she shook her fist at Tilly. Tilly gave a shriek of fear, dropped

DON'T SELL MY HOUSE

the basket of wet laundry, and ran for the outside door. Hands shaking, she yanked it open and raced across the lawn toward her RV.

Slamming the trailer door behind her, Tilly locked it and sank down into a chair, gasping for breath. All at once, the RV started shaking violently, as if someone were pushing against it.

"Don't sell my house!" a voice wailed outside. "Don't sell my house!" Fists began pounding against the door so violently that the metal dented. Tilly fled to the back of the RV and locked herself in the bathroom.

"Don't sell my house," the phantom exclaimed again, shaking the RV until Tilly was sure it would tip over. "If you sell my house, something terrible will happen to your family! Don't sell my house!"

The roar of a car engine pierced the ghost's words. Abruptly, the shaking and pounding ceased. A moment later, Mark and Lisa's car pulled into the driveway. A hysterical Tilly ran out to meet them and told them the whole story.

Mark was upset. As soon as Tilly described the ghost, he recognized her as his dead wife. Until that moment, he had forgotten that he promised his first wife that he would never sell the cottage. But what else could they do? Mark and Lisa needed a bigger house for their growing family, and they could not afford to buy one without selling the cottage.

Mark and Lisa called in their priest to try to appease the spirit of Mark's first wife. The holy man prayed over the cottage and pleaded at length with the photo of the phantom, begging her to release Mark from his promise. The only response he received was the choking smell of expensive perfume, which became so overwhelming that he was forced to leave the cottage until it dissipated.

After much discussion, Mark and Lisa decided to defy the phantom and sell the cottage. Everyone was anxious up to the day of the closing, but nothing further happened. There was no smell of perfume, no rearranging of the furniture, no ectoplasmic appearances. They concluded that the ghost must have listened to the priest and decided to leave them in peace. But Tilly was still nervous. She was the only one to have seen the phantom, and the ghost had not struck Tilly as someone willing to give up easily.

On the night following the family's move from the cottage, Lisa was struck with a terrible pain in her abdomen. Mark rushed her to the hospital, where she gave birth prematurely to the twins, who were stillborn. On his way home from the hospital, Mark's car was struck by a truck, and he was killed instantly. At the same moment, Lisa sat bolt upright in her hospital bed, staring at an empty corner of the room. She screamed once in terror at the sight of the phantom floating before her eyes, and flung up her arms to ward off the specter. Then her eyes rolled back in her head and she fell back on the pillows, dead instantly from a brain aneurism.

Of the three people living on the property when the ghost appeared, Tilly was the only one who survived the ghost's curse. But the overwhelming grief caused by the loss of her family broke her spirit and turned her mind. Within a week after leaving the cottage, Tilly was admitted to an insane asylum, where she spent the rest of her days weeping bitterly and begging her dead daughter not to sell their house.

PART TWO

Powers of Darkness and Light

16

The Birth of the Jersey Devil

Something inside Mother Leeds snapped when she found out she was pregnant yet again; this time with number thirteen. Life was already a struggle with an unreliable and sometimes abusive husband and twelve little children to feed. She worked hard, so very hard, to keep food in her children's stomachs and clothing on their backs. She had not yet managed to put shoes on every foot, but perhaps this last batch of sewing she'd taken in would buy another pair.

Her husband drank away the little money he earned when he felt like working; and more often than not, lately, he did not feel like working at all. A lazy husband might be bearable, for Mother Leeds had enough gumption for two. But the combination of lazy and abusive was not. She spent all the time she wasn't working keeping her children (and herself) away from her husband's ill temper. She had no family and no one to turn to for help, so she remained with her husband and endured.

When her husband arrived home from the tavern in Burlington that evening, Mother Leeds gave him the news with all the gumption and fire she'd had when they first met, before life had become so unbearably hard.

"A curse be on you," she shouted at him fiercely, "for your

indolence and your sloth and your abusive ways! May a curse be on this child, too. May it be a devil to plague you for your sins!"

When Father Leeds raised his hand to her, she ducked under his fist and thrust him out the door with both hands. He fell head over heels, too drunk to catch himself, and landed in the water trough.

"This child will be a devil!" Mother Leeds shouted again, so loudly that the entire neighborhood could hear. "Thirteenth child! Devil's child. And it will come for you first."

Mother Leeds was terrible in her wrath. Her dark eyes blazed almost red in the dim light of the rising thunderstorm. Her arms were spread wide as if she were cursing the whole world, rather than just her good-for-nothing husband. Her children cowered in the back room watching their parents. As Mother Leeds pronounced her curse, a sudden lightning bolt seared a tall pine tree at the edge of the clearing where their small house stood, and a thunderclap shook the house and ground.

She stood unmoving during the burning crash, her long, tangled hair lifting crazily about her wild-eyed figure in the electrified air following the lightning bolt. Father Leeds gave a shout of terror, leapt from the water trough, and fled from the clearing, never to be seen again in the Pinelands.

Mother Leeds went back into her house, as calm as if nothing had happened, and sent her children to bed. All that night and all the next day a terrible storm raged over the Pinelands, flooding the rivers and tearing trees from the ground. But Mother Leeds was serene as she fed the children and sewed the shirts she'd promised to deliver to the local store.

"Will the baby really be a devil, Mama?" her eldest son asked her timidly after a particularly loud thunderclap.

"Yes, my son," she replied calmly. "And you must take your brothers and sisters far away when it is born, or you will suffer the same fate as your father."

The children didn't believe her, of course, but word of the terrible curse swiftly made its way through town and countryside. Folks were hesitant to have any dealings with Mother Leeds, afraid that she might be a witch, but some of the local women stood up for her, knowing what kind of life her husband had given her. The minister spoke to her a few times, asking her if she had any sins she wished to confess to him, but she just smiled calmly, placing a hand on her expanding middle, and said no.

Two months before her thirteenth child was due to be born, Mother Leeds began making arrangements for her children. She secured apprenticeships for the elder boys and housemaid jobs for the older girls. A week before the baby was due, she sent her three youngest children to stay with their eldest sister, who had recently married a local farmer and set up housekeeping in a nearby town.

A storm was raging the night that Mother Leeds was brought to bed in childbirth. The room was full of local women. They had gathered to help her, more out of curiosity than good will, having heard the rumors that Mother Leeds was involved in witchcraft and had sworn she would give birth to a devil. No one believed it, of course, for Mother Leeds still went to church every Sunday, and no harm had come to her when she spoke with the minister. Still, they were curious.

THE BIRTH OF THE JERSEY DEVIL

Tension mounted when the baby finally arrived. It was a relief (and to some a disappointment) when the baby was born completely normal. The midwife cleaned the child and swaddled him in a warm blanket. Turning to hand him to Mother Leeds, she abruptly screamed and dropped the bundle on the floor. The women gasped in horror, but Mother Leeds just watched patiently, knowing what was to come.

The bundle on the floor jerked and writhed, and suddenly the child burst forth from the blanket, changing before their very eyes. He grew larger and larger; hands and feet transforming into claws, wings erupting from his shoulder blades, horns sprouting from his head, and dark eyes glowing with yellow fire like the eyes of a cat. Within minutes, the child was completely grown. Mother Leeds stared in satisfaction at her child, who now resembled a dragon with a head like a horse, the body of a snake, a forked tail, and the wings of a bat.

The more intelligent of the women had taken to their heels the minute the bundle started writhing. Those who remained, horrified and fascinated by the spectacle, immediately got a beating as the devil child's thick forked tail and two enormous wings thrashed about. Even Mother Leeds was not spared a pummeling as she staggered weakly from the bed, still bloody from giving birth. Slowly, she gestured to the chimney.

"You know what you must do," she gasped to the creature.

With a harsh cry, the Leeds Devil flew up the large chimney and vanished into the storm. Lightning struck the blackened stump of pine tree in the same place it had struck the night that Father Leeds had vanished from the Pinelands. A huge clap of thunder shook the house and ground.

When the women had recovered enough from their fear to look around the room, Mother Leeds lay dead beside the chimney. There was a look of peace on her face that the women in the room did not share, for they knew that she had unleashed a Devil upon them all.

They say, though no one knows for sure, that Father Leeds was the first victim of the Jersey Devil. Several of the Leeds children also disappeared in the course of the next few months—those who had not listened to their mother and had taken local jobs rather than leaving the town where they grew up.

Long after all the Leeds family had passed on, the Leeds monster—called the Jersey Devil—continued to haunt the Pinelands of New Jersey; wrecking havoc upon farmers' crops and livestock, poisoning pools and creeks, and appearing on the Jersey shore just before a ship wrecked.

17

La Mala Hora

My friend Isabela called me one evening before dinner. She was sobbing as she told me that she and her husband, Enrique, were getting divorced. He had moved out of the house earlier that day, and Isabela was distraught.

I called my husband, who was on a business trip in Chicago, and he agreed that I should go stay with Isabela for a few days to help her during this difficult time. I packed a small suitcase and got right into the car. It was late, and it would take me at least four hours to drive from my home to Santa Fe. Isabela was expecting me to arrive around midnight. As I traveled down the dark, wet highway, I could not shake the feeling that someone or something was watching me. I kept looking in the rearview mirror and glancing into the backseat. No one was there. *Don't be ridiculous*, I told myself, wishing fervently that I was home in my bed instead of driving on a dark, rainy night. There was almost no traffic, so I sped up the car, eager to reach Santa Fe.

I turned off the highway just before I entered the city and started down the side roads that led to Isabela's house. As I approached a small crossroads, I saw a woman step into the street directly in front of my car. I shrieked in fright and slammed on my brakes, praying I would miss her.

LA MALA HORA

The car skidded to a halt, and I looked frantically around for the woman. Then I saw her, right beside my window, looking in at me. She had the face of a demon, twisted, eyes glowing red, and short, pointed teeth.

I screamed as she leapt at my window, her clawed hands striking the glass. I jammed my foot down on the accelerator and the car lurched forward. For a few terrible moments, she ran alongside the vehicle, keeping up easily and striking at me again and again.

Finally she fell behind, but in the rearview mirror I saw her growing taller and taller, until she was as large as a tree. Red light swirled around her like mist, and she pointed in my direction, her mouth moving, though I could not make out the words. I jerked my attention back to the road, afraid of what might happen to me if my car ran off the street.

I made it to Isabela's house in record time and flung myself out of the car, pounding on her door frantically and looking behind me to see if the demon-faced woman had followed me. Isabela came running to the door and let me in.

"Shut the door! Shut it!" I cried frantically, brushing past her into the safety of the house.

"Jane, what's wrong?" she asked, slamming the door shut. She grabbed my hand and led me into the living room. I sank onto the couch and started sobbing in fear and shock. After several minutes, I managed to stammer out my story. Isabela gasped and said, "Are you sure you were at a crossroads when you saw her?"

I nodded, puzzled by her question.

"It must have been La Mala Hora," Isabela said, wringing her hands.

"The evil hour?" I asked, interpreting the Spanish as best I could.

"This is bad, Jane. Very bad," Isabela cried. "La Mala Hora only appears at a crossroads when someone is going to die."

Ordinarily, I would have laughed at such a superstition, but the appearance of the demon-woman had shaken me. Isabela got me a cup of hot cocoa, brought my luggage in from the car, and sent me to bed. She was so concerned for me that she didn't once mention the divorce or Enrique.

I felt much better the next morning, but I could not shake the feeling of dread that grew within me all day. Neither of us mentioned La Mala Hora, but we were both thinking of her when I told Isabela that I wanted to go home. I flatly refused to drive after dark, afraid I would see the demon-woman again, so I spent one more night in Santa Fe.

We left the next morning and Isabela insisted on accompanying me. We hadn't been home more than twenty minutes when a police car pulled into my driveway. I knew at once what it meant, and so did Isabela.

The officers spoke very gently to me, but nothing could soften the news. My husband had been mugged on the way back to his hotel after dinner the previous night. His body had not been found until this morning. He had been shot in the head and died instantly.

18

Bloody Bones

Way back in the deep woods there lived a scrawny old woman who had a reputation for being the best conjuring woman in the Ozarks. With her bedraggled black-and-gray hair, funny eyes—one yellow and one green—and her crooked nose, Old Betty was not a pretty picture, but she was the best there was at fixing what ailed a man—and that was all that mattered.

Old Betty's house was full of herbs and roots and bottles filled with conjuring medicine. The walls were lined with strange books brimming with magical spells. Old Betty was the only one living in the Hollow who knew how to read; her granny, who was also a conjurer, had taught her the skill as part of her magical training.

Folks coming to Old Betty for a cure to their ailment sometimes peeked through the window beside her rickety porch, curious to see what was inside a conjure-woman's house. Old Betty never invited anyone in, and no one would have gone inside if she had.

Just about the only friend Old Betty had was a tough, mean, ugly old razorback hog that ran wild around her place. It rooted so much in her kitchen garbage that all the leftover spells started affecting it. Some folks swore up and down that the old razorback hog sometimes walked upright like a man. One fellow claimed he'd seen the pig sitting in the rocker on Old Betty's porch, chattering away to her while she stewed up some potions in the kitchen, but everyone discounted that story on account of the fellow who told it was a little too fond of moonshine.

"Raw Head" was the name Old Betty gave the razorback, referring maybe to the way the ugly creature looked a bit like some of the dead pigs you could see come butchering time down in Hog-Scald Hollow. The razorback didn't mind the funny name. Raw Head kept following Old Betty around her little cabin and rooting up the kitchen leftovers. He'd even walk to town with her when she went to the local mercantile to sell her home remedies.

Well, folks got so used to seeing Raw Head and Old Betty in the town that it looked mighty strange one day around hog-driving time when Old Betty came to the mercantile without him.

"Where's Raw Head?" the owner asked as he accepted her basket full of home-remedy potions.

The liquid in the bottles swished in an agitated manner as Old Betty said, "I ain't seen him around today and I'm mighty worried. You seen him here in town?"

"Nobody's seen him around today. They would've told me if they did," the mercantile owner said. "We'll keep a lookout fer you."

"That's mighty kind of you. If you see him, tell him to come home straightaway," Old Betty said. The mercantile owner nodded in agreement as he handed over her weekly pay.

BLOODY BONES

Old Betty fussed to herself all the way home. It wasn't like Raw Head to disappear, especially not on the day they went to town. The man at the mercantile always saved the best scraps for the mean old razorback, and Raw Head never missed a visit. When the old conjuring woman got home, she mixed up a potion and poured it onto a flat plate.

"Where's that old hog gone to?" she asked the liquid. It clouded over and then a series of pictures formed. First, Old Betty saw the good-for-nothing hunter that lived on the next ridge sneaking around the forest, rounding up razorback hogs that didn't belong to him. One of the hogs was Raw Head. She saw him taking the hogs down to Hog-Scald Hollow, where folks from the next town were slaughtering their razorbacks. Then she saw her own hog, Raw Head, slaughtered with the rest of the pigs and hung up for gutting! The final picture in the liquid was the pile of bloody bones that had once been her hog, and his scraped-clean head lying with the other hogs' heads in a pile.

Old Betty was infuriated. It was murder to her, plain and simple. Everyone in three counties knew that Raw Head was her friend, and that lazy, hog-stealing, good-for-nothing hunter on the ridge was going to pay for slaughtering him.

Now Old Betty tried to practice white magic most of the time, but she knew the dark secrets, too. She pulled out an old, secret book her granny had given her and turned to the very last page. She lit several candles and put them around the plate containing the liquid picture of Raw Head and his bloody bones. Then she began to chant: "Raw Head and Bloody Bones. Raw Head and Bloody Bones."

The light from the windows disappeared as if the sun had been snuffed out like a candle. Dark clouds billowed into the clearing where Old Betty's cabin stood, and the howl of dark spirits could be heard in the wind that pummeled the treetops.

"Raw Head and Bloody Bones. Raw Head and Bloody Bones."

Betty continued the chant until a bolt of silver lightning left the plate and streaked out through the window, heading in the direction of Hog-Scald Hollow.

When the silver light struck Raw Head's severed head, which was piled on the hunter's wagon with the other hog heads, it tumbled to the ground and rolled until it was touching the bloody bones that had once inhabited its body. As the hunter's wagon rumbled away toward the ridge where he lived, the enchanted Raw Head called out: "Bloody bones, get up and dance!"

Immediately, the bloody bones reassembled themselves into the skeleton of a razorback hog walking upright, as Raw Head had often done when he was alone with Old Betty. The head hopped on top of his skeleton, and Raw Head went searching through the woods for weapons to use against the hunter. He borrowed the sharp teeth of a dying panther, the claws of a long-dead bear, and the tail from a rotting raccoon and put them over his skinned head and bloody bones.

Then Raw Head headed up the track toward the ridge, looking for the hunter who had slaughtered him. Raw Head slipped passed the thief on the road and slid into the barn where the hunter kept his horse and wagon. He climbed up into the loft and waited for the hunter to arrive.

It was dusk when the hunter drove into the barn and unhitched his horse. The horse snorted in fear, sensing the presence of Raw Head in the loft. Wondering what was disturbing his usually calm horse, the hunter looked around and saw a large pair of eyes staring down at him from the darkness above.

The hunter frowned, thinking it was one of the local kids fooling around in his barn.

"Land o' goshen, what have you got those big eyes fer?" he snapped, thinking the kids were trying to scare him with some crazy mask.

"To see your grave," Raw Head mumbled very softly. The hunter snorted irritably and put his horse into the stall.

"Very funny. Ha, ha," The hunter said. When he came out of the stall, he saw Raw Head had crept forward a bit further. Now his luminous yellow eyes and his bear claws could clearly be seen.

"Land o' goshen, what have you got those big claws fer?" he snapped. "You look ridiculous."

"To dig your grave," Raw Head intoned softly, his voice a deep rumble that raised the hairs on the back of the hunter's neck. He stirred uneasily, not sure how the crazy kid in his loft could have made such a scary sound—if it really was a crazy kid.

Feeling a little spooked, he hurried to the door and let himself out of the barn. Raw Head slipped off the loft and climbed down the side of the barn behind him. With nary a rustle, Raw Head raced through the trees and up the path to a large, moonlit rock. He hid in the shadow of the stone so that the only things showing were his gleaming yellow eyes, his bear claws, and his raccoon tail.

When the hunter came level with the rock on the side of the path, he gave a startled yelp. Staring at Raw Head, he gasped: "You nearly knocked the heart right out of me, you crazy kid! Land o' goshen, what have you got that crazy tail fer?"

"To sweep your grave," Raw Head boomed, his enchanted voice echoing through the woods, getting louder and louder with each echo.

At this point, the hunter took to his heels and ran for his cabin. He raced past the old well-house, past the wood pile, over the rotting fence, and into his yard. But Raw Head was faster. When the hunter reached his porch, Raw Head leapt from the shadows and loomed above him. The hunter stared in terror up at Raw Head's gleaming yellow eyes, his bloody bone skeleton with its long bear claws, sweeping raccoon's tail, and his razor-sharp panther teeth.

"Land o' goshen, what have you got those big teeth fer?" he gasped desperately, stumbling backward from the terrible figure before him.

"To eat you up, like you wanted to eat me!" Raw Head roared, descending upon the good-for-nothing hunter. The murdering thief gave one long scream in the moonlight. Then there was nothing but silence, broken by the sound of crunching.

Nothing more was ever seen or heard of the lazy hunter who lived on the ridge. His horse also disappeared that night. But sometimes folks would see Raw Head roaming through the forest in the company of his friend Old Betty. And once a month, on the night of the full moon, Raw Head would ride the hunter's horse through town, wearing the old man's blue overalls over his bloody bones with a hole cut out for his raccoon tail. In his bloody, bear-clawed hands, he carried his raw, razorback hog's head, lifting it high against the full moon for everyone to see.

19

I Can't Get In

We attended the local dance together, my pal Arnie and I, and we made quite a splash among the fair ladies, if I do say so myself. What with the pretty company and the illicit moonshine they were serving in the punch, Arnie and I ended the evening a little worse for wear. (That moonshine was *strong*!)

"Do you remember how to get home?" I asked Arnie blurrily. There were at least three Arnies warring for dominance in my vision. I addressed my question to the middle one, but it was the one on the far right who answered me.

"S-sure I do," Arnie said cheerfully, "Just f-follow me, Jack!"

He headed out the door in the wrong direction; at least, I was pretty sure it was the wrong direction. I caught him by the arm and spun him around before he walked into the river. The sudden twist turned his broad red face an interesting shade of green. The sight of his queasiness made my stomach start to feel funny, too.

"Let's go this way," I suggested, pointing toward the road in front of the dance hall.

"G-great idea," Arnie said and plunged forward—literally. I picked him up from the ground, dusted him off a bit, and carefully negotiated my way around the large root that had tripped him up. Then we were free and clear, walking down the blurry road toward our homes, which stood side by side on the other end of the neighborhood.

You know, I never knew how much effort walking took. Getting one foot in front of the other and sending them both in the direction I intended—while not bumping them into obstacles—was quite a challenge that night.

"You know, Jackie my friend, I think maybe we're a tad d-drunk," Arnie said to me as he walked into a low-hanging branch on the side of the road.

"Do tell," I invited, catching him before he fell over again.

"I am telling you," Arnie said, blinking owlishly at me. "Say, you're not looking too good."

This was an understatement. Every thud of my feet against the ground was making my stomach do flip-flops, and my head felt as if a few dozen drummers had taken up residence inside. If I had a mirror (which, thank God, I did not), I was sure my complexion would have been a sickly shade of green. As it was, I felt pale and sweaty and not well.

"Let's just get home, quick," I said to Arnie, who nodded in complete understanding. He was a much larger guy than I was, standing well over six feet tall and built like a linebacker, so the moonshine hadn't hit him quite as hard as a medium-sized string bean like me. At least, not yet!

"We can cut through the graveyard and save ten minutes," Arnie suggested, pointing to the left.

I peered intently into the darkness. Things were still criss-crossing and blurring in front of my eyes, but I finally made out the distinctly cut shapes of some tombstones and at least one mausoleum. The local graveyard was fairly well-tended, with gravel paths and nicely cut grass and just enough shade trees to make it a pleasant place to visit the recently departed—during the daytime. At night, the shadows deepened and darted mysteriously hither and thither among the stones, as if they had a life of their own. And the wind moaned through the trees, rustling the leaves until they sounded like the voices of the dead.

"I ain't going in there," I said firmly, turning away with an air of finality and knocking myself in the head with the same branch that had just beaned Arnie. The drubbing did not help my poor, aching head one bit.

"Oh, yes you are," said Arnie, taking me by the arm and walking us both right back into the low-hanging tree branch. We picked each other up off the ground and staggered into the graveyard.

"Spooooooky," I whispered to Arnie, getting rather carried away on my "oo" sound. He must have liked the tone, because he repeated my comment, and his booming voice echoed strangely within the mausoleum on our right.

I know I said there were nice gravel paths in the local graveyard, but Arnie and I didn't find any that night. We just wove our way through the graves, walking all over the good, dead folk of our village in our determination to get home in one piece.

I don't know which was spinning more, my head or my stomach, but all at once, I knew I couldn't go on. We'd reached the middle of the graveyard, and I couldn't move a step further

I CAN'T GET IN

without being sick. Motioning Arnie to keep going, I dodged behind a tombstone and quietly got rid of all the food I'd eaten at the dance. Staggering away from the smelly mess I'd made, I sank down on a handy grave and leaned back against the tombstone to rest.

I could hear Arnie humming to himself as he climbed over the ornamental iron fence that surrounded the graveyard and fell face down on the pavement on the far side, right next to the open gate. The whole world was still shaking slightly, and my stomach was still tetchy, so I stayed where I was as Arnie staggered to his feet and continued on down the road.

Suddenly, I felt a bony tap on my shoulder. It was so unexpected that I gave a shriek of surprise and whipped my head around to look behind me. I was expecting another low-hanging branch, but what met my gaze was something much worse. A tall, gleaming white skeleton with a flickering blue light glowing in its eye sockets was gazing down on me from beside the tombstone.

"Excuse me, young man," the skeleton said politely.

"Wha . . . wha . . . wha . . . " I replied hoarsely, unable to catch my breath.

"You appear to be sitting on my grave," the skeleton continued.

"Wha . . . wha . . . wha . . . " I said, staring bug-eyed with fear. My heart was thundering in my chest, and my muscles were frozen stiff.

"Can you hear me?" asked the skeleton, waving a bony hand in front of my eyes. "I said, you are sitting on my grave, and I can't get in."

"Wha . . . wha . . . wha . . . " I gasped.

The skeleton leaned down until his bony face and the blazing blue lights that were his eye sockets were right in front of me.

"I said," it repeated slowly and patiently, as if it were speaking to a very daft person, "you are in my way, and I can't get into my grave."

That did it.

"Waaaaaaaaaaaaaaaaaaa!" I screamed, leaping up from the grave and fleeing for my life. Faintly, just above the sound of my screams and pounding feet, I heard the skeleton mutter, "Really, young people these days. No respect for the dead." Then it climbed back into its grave.

I passed Arnie on the road and kept right on going. Eventually, I collapsed on my front porch, clinging to the railing with both hands as I caught my breath. I was stone-cold sober and shaking like a leaf when Arnie caught up with me.

"What happened?" he shouted. "You look like you've seen a ghost."

"No, just a skeleton," I replied, laughing hysterically in fear and relief. Then I told him the whole story. He didn't believe me, of course, even though I swore on a stack of Bibles that it was true. Told me I was drunk and imagined the whole thing, which of course might have been the truth of the matter. Still, I never walked through that graveyard again, just in case.

20

The Werewolf's Bride

She was a high-spirited beauty who was the toast of the regiment, and he was a poor foot soldier without two pennies to rub together. They should never have met at all, if the soldier had not chanced upon her one day while making his rounds. Her dress had been caught by a briar bush, and she was endeavoring in vain to free herself. The soldier rushed to her aid. When he had freed her, the soldier gazed into her deep blue eyes as she smiled and thanked him—and he lost his heart forever.

To his amazement, the soldier soon learned that his affections were returned. At the next town social, she would dance with no one but him, and she invited him to dinner to meet her parents. For a few days, there was some jealousy and sour faces among the men in his regiment, but their attitudes changed when the men observed the powerful love that had sprung up between the soldier and his lady.

Now the soldier's beautiful girl had caught the eye of an evil woodsman who had sold his soul in exchange for the ability to turn himself into a wolf at will. One evening, the woodsman crouched down in the woods and waited for the girl as she was walking home. He accosted her roughly, demanding that she elope with him. The maiden refused, spurning his love and crying out for someone to save her.

The girl's cries were heard by her fiancé, who had come searching when she was late returning to her parents' home. The soldier drove the woodsman away with harsh words, threatening him with dire consequences if he ever approached the maiden again.

The furious woodsman laid low for a few weeks, waiting for his chance. It came on the girl's wedding day. She was dancing happily at her wedding reception with a group of her friends when the woodsman, in the form of a wolf, leapt upon her and dragged her away.

The enraged bridegroom gave chase, but the wolf and the bride disappeared deep into the thick forest and were not seen again.

For many days, the distraught soldier and his friends— armed with silver bullets that could kill a werewolf—scoured the woods in search of the maiden and her captor. At one point, the soldier thought he saw the wolf and shot at it. Upon reaching the location, he found a piece of a wolf's tail lying on the ground, but there was no sign of the wolf to which it belonged.

Months of searching ensued, and eventually the soldier's friends begged him to let the girl go and get on with his life. But the soldier was half-mad with grief and refused to give up. And that very day, he found the cave where the werewolf lived. Within it lay the body of his beloved bride. The girl had refused the werewolf's advances to the very end and had died because of that.

THE WEREWOLF'S BRIDE

Once his murderous fury had faded away, the werewolf had tenderly laid the body of the girl he had loved and killed into a wooden coffin, where it would be safe from predators. The werewolf came to visit her remains every day.

Enraged, the soldier hid and waited for his enemy to return. As soon as the werewolf entered the cavern, the man shot at it over and over again. Blinded by pain, the werewolf fled from the cave, but the angry soldier stayed right on his heels. With a howl of terror, the dying werewolf leapt into a nearby lake and disappeared from view.

The soldier sat by the lake, cradling his gun and waiting for the werewolf to surface so he could finish him off. But the water was still, save for the little ripples blown by the wind. As the soldier watched, bloody pieces of the dead werewolf began to float to the surface of the water. These parts were quickly consumed by the ever-present catfish.

When his friends from the regiment finally tracked him down, the soldier's mind was gone. He babbled insanely about a werewolf that had been eaten by catfish, and he sobered just long enough to lead the men to the body of his beloved. Then the soldier collapsed forevermore into insanity. He died a few days later and was buried beside his bride in a little glen where they had planned to build their home.

Their graves are long forgotten, and the place where the couple rest is covered with daisies in the spring. But to this day, the people of the area have a prejudice against eating catfish, though no one remembers why.

21

Cow's Head

Oksana lived in a small house on the edge of town with her father and her soon-to-be stepmother and stepsister. Her father's new wife was incredibly jealous of the poor girl and deeply resented her, favoring her true daughter, Olena, instead.

Within a month after her father's remarriage, Oksana found that all the housework fell to her while Olena idled her days away. Oksana's father was a timid man, and he could not bring himself to defy his wife. So Oksana wore Olena's cast-off clothes, and her hands grew red and chapped from scrubbing in the cold, while Olena attended parties, rubbed rich lotions into her soft hands, and grew more lazy and spoiled every day.

One year, when the winter snows were particularly fierce, Oksana's family ran out of money. Oksana's stepmother began nagging her husband to send his daughter away, telling him that they could not afford to keep two girls. Reluctantly, Oksana's father agreed. He took Oksana to a cottage deep in the woods and left her there.

Oksana was very frightened. The woods were said to be filled with demons and monsters. But Oksana was also practical. She entered the cottage with her small bundle and found a fireplace, a lopsided table, and a rusty old pot. Oksana put away the loaf of bread, the knife, and the slab of cheese her father had given her. She folded her blanket and lay it near the fireplace. Then she collected wood from the surrounding forest and built a fire.

Oksana knew the bread and cheese would not last for long. So she made a snare using the thin, flexible branches of the trees and caught a snow rabbit to eat. She also dug under the deep snow and found some roots and berries for food.

By dark, Oksana had melted snow for drinking water and used the rest of the water to make a stew. So Oksana ate well. Then she lay down near the fire for the night, listening to the wind howl and telling herself that she was not frightened of the woods.

It was midnight when the knock came.

Knock, knock, knock.

It echoed hollowly through the dark cottage. Oksana woke with a start, her heart pounding in fear. It came again.

Knock, knock, knock.

Oksana thought of the monsters. She hid under her blanket, praying whatever it was would go away.

Knock, knock, knock.

Oksana rose, grabbing a branch. She crept toward the door. The wind howled eerily down the chimney. Oksana swallowed and quickly swung the door open.

There was nothing there. Her heart pounded fiercely as she stared out at the snow whipping about in the light of her small fire. Then she looked down. Oksana let out a shriek of terror and leapt back, dropping her stick. It was a demon—an evil spirit.

And it had no body!

"Who are you?" Oksana stuttered, clutching the door with shaking hands.

"I am Cow's Head," it replied, solemnly.

Indeed, Oksana saw at once that it was. The head was brown, with curved horns and strange, haunted eyes.

"I am cold and hungry. May I sleep by your fire?" Cow's Head asked. Its voice was cold and lifeless.

Oksana gulped down her horror.

"Of course," she said.

"Lift me over the threshold," demanded Cow's Head hollowly. Oksana did as she was ordered.

"Place me near the fire."

Anger warred with compassion inside her, but compassion won. Oksana put it next to the fire.

"I am hungry," said Cow's Head. "Feed me."

Oksana thought of her meager food supply. The stew left in the pot was for her breakfast. She fed it to Cow's Head.

"I will sleep now," it said. There was no softening in its attitude toward her. Nonetheless, Oksana made it comfortable for the night, giving it her blanket and sleeping in a cold corner with only her cloak to keep her warm.

When she woke in the morning, Cow's Head was gone. Where it had slept was a large trunk, filled with the most beautiful gowns she had ever seen. Under the gowns lay heaps of gold and jewels.

Oksana stared blankly at the riches in front of her. And then, out of the blue, a knock on the door and a man's voice startled her. She whipped around to see her father standing there.

COW'S HEAD

"Daughter, I have come," he said softly.

Oksana forgot the trunk in her joy. She ran into his arms. He had defied her stepmother to come and bring her back to their home. But then she remembered the beautiful goods and excitedly showed them to her father.

"Papa, come see!" Oksana exclaimed as she pulled him into the cottage. Her words tumbled over each other as she explained.

Her father was delighted by her news and took her home. There, Oksana was honored in her town for her compassion and her bravery, and won scores of suitors. She married soon after her return from the cottage.

Hearing Oksana's story, and seeing the riches she had received, Olena went to the cottage in the forest and spent the night there. But when Cow's Head appeared, she was too lazy to serve it. In the morning, all her gowns had turned to rags— and her possessions to dust.

But Oksana lived to a ripe old age in happiness and prosperity.

22

Tom Dunn's Dance

Tom Dunn was a rascal of a fellow who would rather drink and dance than go to church, but he was a favorite with the ladies, being tall and handsome. Tom went to all the social events, and was very popular. Still, the minister and the deacons all shook their heads over his behavior, fearing for his immortal soul if he kept up his rascally ways.

One fine night Tom attended the local husking bee. He was in high spirits that night, for there was plenty to drink, and he had a pretty partner. The only low point came when the minister took him aside for a few moments to talk about his immortal soul and the mending of his ways. But a few drinks cured Tom of his uneasiness, and after he had shucked twenty red ears of corn and claimed twenty kisses from his pretty partner as payment for them, Tom was on top of the world. Feeling self-satisfied and rather reckless, he decided to take a shortcut home, even though it meant going over Rag Rock at night.

Now, everyone knew that Rag Rock was the home of terrible spirits and many demon-kind. Legend said that underneath Rag Rock, an evil spirit was holding the Indian maiden Nansema and her lover Winitihooloo captive inside a glittering cave filled with treasure. Tom Dunn usually avoided Rag Rock, wanting nothing to do with demons or with angels for that matter, not being fond of anything spiritual in nature. But on this night Tom just laughed at the old tales and went straight up the hill.

As Tom neared the top of Rag Rock, he heard the sound of a fiddle floating on the breeze. A light appeared among the trees, and he could hear laughter and the sound of feet shuffling in a dance.

Oh no, he said to himself. It seems that some of the so-called righteous townsfolk have got themselves up a moonlight dance. The minister should see this. After hearing the sacrilegious music they're playing, he won't be so quick to tell me I'm shaming the town.

Tom pushed his way through the thicket, eager to see whom he had caught making merry on Rag Rock. A moment later he found himself on the edge of a clearing. Torches flared on every side, and there was a joyous crowd milling about and dancing in a spirited manner quite unlike any he had ever seen.

Now, Tom dearly enjoyed a good dance, and this one was better than the best of its kind. His toes tapped to the cheery fiddle tune as he gazed about in wonder. Then he gave a delighted laugh and strode boldly into the ring of dancers. He offered them an elaborate bow, and they greeted him with a friendly shout.

A girl with laughing black eyes and rosy red lips was sitting just outside the circle. She eyed him mischievously and twitched her skirt, allowing him to catch a glimpse of her pretty ankles. The invitation in her eyes and her flirtatious sidelong glance were all the incentive Tom needed to sweep her

TOM DUNN'S DANCE

out of her seat and into the dance. Tom whirled her about in the wildest dance he had ever led. He seemed to be floating in the air, so light were his heels and so dashing his moves.

Soon an admiring ring had formed around Tom and his partner, inciting him to new heights and marvelous feats of skill. The fiddle seemed to put lightning in his heels; he could make no wrong move this night. He swung his partner around and they separated in order to dance back to each other across the field. Tom gave a mighty leap and a whirl, cracking his heels together. As he came to the ground, he noticed that his partner, who was dancing suggestively toward him, had changed. She looked older; her face had grown longer and her eyes were dark and hard. Tom twirled again, and now when he came face to face with his partner, he saw with dismay that she had transformed completely. Her form was lank and twisted, her hair wild and disarrayed, her teeth yellow and pointed, and her green eyes full of wickedness and glee.

In that moment Tom realized that he was in the company of the demon inhabitants of Rag Rock. His partner gave him a twisted smile as they joined hands, and the faces in the crowd were no longer noble, though they were still merry. Tom was trembling with such fear that his legs would barely hold him. But he knew if he stopped dancing now, his fate was sealed. The only way out for him was to dance until sunrise, or for a minister to order him to stop. But his minister was safe in bed, and Tom knew he had to dance or die.

Well, the fat was in the fire. Tom threw off his coat and tie and settled into a steady jig, fancy antics forgotten. The moon was setting over the trees. If he could hold out for two more hours, he would be free.

His partner giggled happily and tried to snuggle up to him, but he danced away from her. He could not escape the others so easily. Each way he turned, another gleaming pair of evil eyes, or a face not quite human, was watching him. Many of the demon-folk raised their glasses to him in a threatening toast.

By this time Tom was in agony. His muscles burned and his body was shaking with fatigue. *I must keep dancing,* he told himself, urging himself on. No one else was dancing now. They were all watching him hungrily. The clearing was silent except for the obscenely merry sound of the fiddle.

Suddenly a cramp caught Tom in the calf. He doubled over in agony, and his onetime partner shouted with glee. She loomed above him, and a whiff of sulfur choked him. "God save me," shouted Tom, tumbling onto his back.

At the name of God, there came a sudden hissing sound. Tom heard growls and curses and had a brief vision of inhuman figures scurrying away. The witch, who was hanging greedily over him, burst into flames. The stink of sulfur and the blazing flames overwhelmed him, and Tom knew no more.

He woke at daybreak. He was lying in the dirt of an overgrown clearing, his coat and his tie next to him. His head pounded fiercely.

"Lord, what a hangover," he moaned, pushing himself up. "And what a terrible dream."

His jackknife fell out of his pocket as he spoke. He bent painfully to pick it up, then immediately dropped it with a terrified gasp. The face of the pretty girl with whom he had danced was etched on the handle. Kneeling down in the dirt, he picked up the knife again. Yes, it was she. Slowly he turned the knife over. On the other side was the picture of the witch as she'd looked right before he blacked out.

Feeling sick and feverish, Tom thrust the knife into his pocket, grabbed his things, and stumbled his way home. He lay in bed for a month with fever. When his health returned,

Tom immediately joined the church, married his pretty partner from the husking bee, forsook all worldly entertainments, and never drank anything stronger than tea. The minister was delighted that Tom had taken his speech to heart, and ever afterward claimed credit for Tom's reformation.

Within a few years Tom was a deacon and was considered by all to be the most honest and upright workman in the community. If at times he vexed his wife with his refusal to attend any of the village dances, he was in all other respects a model husband. When he died, his wife put up a grand tombstone in his honor.

23

The Death Coach

It was midnight, and the streets of Cohoes grew silent as the citizens turned off their lights, one by one, and went to their well-earned resting places. The night was dark, and the wind whispered softly, touching the trees and houses and rattling a windowpane here and there.

In the house at the center of the street, a small, careworn woman sat at the bedside of her husband, who tossed and turned among the blankets. He had been bitten by a poisonous snake that afternoon, and his fever had climbed so high that he did not know who she was. The woman had sent a neighbor for the doctor, who had come immediately with some antivenom medication. The doctor had given her careful instructions for her husband's care and she had followed them to the letter, but her husband grew worse and worse as day turned to night.

The doctor had promised to come to them again when he finished his daily rounds, and the woman anxiously listened for the sound of his carriage as she applied cool cloths to her husband's forehead. His fever was still climbing, and she was afraid that his mind might be permanently damaged by the poison.

Her husband's face grew paler as he shook with cold. There was pain in the gray lines around his mouth. The pain was something new, and she did not have anything to give him to make it go away. She clutched her husband's hand tightly, praying as hard as she could that his life would be spared.

A part of her knew that her husband was slipping away. He could not have such a high fever and live. No one could. And the raking pain that struck through his body again and again was horrific. She wanted to scream out in desperation, begging him not to leave her alone, but he would not have heard her anyway.

Outside the house, the soft rumble of wheels and the clip-clop of hooves echoed through the still night. The woman tore her eyes from her husband's face and turned in relief. At last, the doctor was coming. She hurried to the window and looked outside, expecting to see the doctor's curricle pulling into the street. Instead, she saw a dark, closed coach with black, gaping holes where the windows should be. The shafts at the front of the coach were empty, yet she could hear the sound of horses' hooves as the coach moved slowly down the street.

She drew in a deep, terrified breath. Long ago, her grandmother had told her about the dark coach that traveled the lonely streets every night, invisible to all save those who had an appointment with its driver. It was the Death Coach.

"No," she whispered softly, and then repeated the word as loud as she could. Death would not—could not—come for her husband. Not yet. Not now. He was too young. They had their whole lives ahead of them.

THE DEATH COACH

As she watched, the dark coach rolled slowly up to their house and stopped by the front gate. The door opened, and a shrouded figure emerged. Its dark robes swirled as if caught in a ghostly wind, and the face under the hood was merely a skull with glowing red eyes that looked straight up at her. She gasped in terror as the dark figure raised an arm and pointed a skeletal finger at the window.

Behind her, her husband gave a great gasp. She whirled in time to see his body convulse once, twice. She leapt to his side and pulled him into her arms. "Don't leave me," she shouted. "Don't leave me."

But her husband was dead before his body hit the pillows, his eyes wide open and unseeing, the lines of pain still on his white, sweat-covered face.

"No," she screamed. "*No!*"

She shook his lifeless body, trying to make him come back to her. Then she ran back to the window and looked outside.

Below her, she saw the front door open and the spirit of her husband step out onto the front porch and walk slowly down the path to the Death Coach. The dark skeleton bowed and opened the door of the coach as her husband approached, shutting it firmly behind him once he stepped inside.

The dark figure turned and looked up at the window where she stood. She and the wraith stared at each other for a long moment. Then the figure vanished as if it had never been there, and the Death Coach rumbled down the street, turned a corner, and was gone.

"Goodbye, my love," she gasped softly, overcome with tears. She sank to the floor, weeping quietly as the rattle of another carriage echoed down the lane. It was the doctor—he had come a moment too late to check on his patient. With a heavy heart, the woman stood, shut the window, and went down the stairs to tell him that her husband was dead.

24

The Hook

The reports had been on the radio all day, though Jane hadn't paid much attention to them. Some crazy man had escaped from the state asylum. They were calling him the Hook Man because he had lost his right arm and had it replaced with a hook. He was a serial killer, and everyone in the region was warned to keep watch and report anything suspicious. But this didn't interest Jane in the slightest. What did madmen have to do with her? She had more pressing matters on her mind, like what she should wear on her date with Matt.

After several hours of hemming and hawing, Jane chose a smashing off-the-shoulder affair in the very latest style and spent an hour curling her long dark hair. Finally, she was ready to go, and just in time, too. She heard Matt's car pull up outside and went to meet him on the porch.

"Don't stay out past curfew!" her father warned lazily from his place on the porch swing.

"Of course not, sir," Matt said. He was always the perfect gentleman in front of her father.

They turned the radio up and sang along to their favorite CD as they cruised up the mountain to the local drive-in theater. The place was a madhouse, and they laughed and ate popcorn and traded jokes with several other couples who had parked in the same vicinity. It was a wonderful evening.

When the movie was through, Matt eyeballed Jane and slyly suggested that they drive to the nearby overlook to take in the view. Jane grinned back at him, happy to do a little necking with her favorite fellow. The blue outfit was definitely a hit. Jane made a mental note to buy a few more off-the-shoulder dresses as she cuddled close to her boyfriend in the darkened car. They'd tuned into a local radio station and spent some time necking to the sound of romantic music in the background.

Then the announcer came on and repeated the warning Jane had heard that afternoon. An insane killer with a hook in place of his right hand was loose in the area. She stiffened in Matt's arms, vividly conscious of their remote location on top of the hill. Suddenly, the dark, moonless night didn't seem so romantic to her. The overlook was secluded and off the beaten track, after all. *A perfect spot for a deranged madman to lurk,* Jane thought, pushing her amorous boyfriend away.

"I don't like the sound of that announcement," Jane said nervously. "Maybe we should get out of here? That Hook Man sounds dangerous."

"Aww, c'mon babe, it's nothing," Matt said, trying to get in another kiss. She pushed him away again.

"No, really. We're all alone out here. I'm scared," she said.

"I'll protect you," Matt said confidently, taking her back into his arms. But Jane was no longer in the mood for romance. She was scared and made no bones about it.

THE HOOK

The couple argued for a moment more, but then the car shook a bit—as if something . . . or someone . . . had pressed against it. Jane gave a shriek, "Get us out of here *now*!"

"Jeez," Matt said in disgust, "just like a girl!"

With a sour expression on his face, he turned the key and went roaring out of the lover's lane with a screeching of tires.

They drove home in stony silence, Matt occasionally muttering to himself about the crazy notions of girls. Jane ignored him, just happy that they'd gotten away from that secluded spot.

When they pulled into her driveway, Matt refused to help her out of the car; a small courtesy he usually paid her. *Typical male*, Jane fumed. He was being so unreasonable.

She opened the door indignantly and stepped into her driveway with her chin up and her lips set. Whirling around, she slammed the door as hard as she could. And then she screamed.

Matt leapt out of the car, his ire forgotten in concern, and raced around the engine to her side of the car. Catching Jane in his arms, he cried, "What is it? What's wrong?" Then he saw it.

A bloody hook hung from the handle of the passenger-side door, wrenched from the arm of the raving lunatic who had been stalking them on top of the hill.

25

Shadow Train

A miner was on his way to Dos Cabezas, where he'd heard there was good prospecting, when he found himself lost and alone in the flats just north of the Dragoon Mountains. In the blistering sun of midday, his burro dropped dead from heatstroke. The prospector knew that he would shortly follow if he didn't find shelter and something to drink soon.

The landscape wobbled before his eyes, and he staggered forward, determined not to drop. But the heat of the desert flats seeped into his body, and he found his wits wandering. The last sensible thought that crossed his mind before he collapsed was the sorrow his mother would feel when he failed to return home from his journey.

He was awakened by a steady chug-chug sound. Raising his head from the hard, dusty ground, he looked blurrily around him. It sounded like a train was approaching. But that was impossible. There were no tracks in this inhospitable location, and no town for miles. *Clackity-clack. Clackity-clack.* The sound came again, louder this time. *Chug-chug-chug. Clackity-clack.* Then the hiss of steam from an engine. *I'm hallucinating,* he decided to himself.

The miner lay his head on his arms and waited for death to

come. As he broiled in the heat, he began to remember the words of the old-timer from whom he had learned of the good prospecting sites in the north. The grizzled man had spoken of a shadow train that sometimes came bursting out of nowhere and ran just above the flats where no railroad tracks had ever lain. Once the shadow train had sped across the desert right before the old man's eyes; a dark smudge against the dazzling light of noonday. It had vanished into the distance while the old man watched, wavering into mirage and then vanishing into the dazzle of the sun.

When he first heard the old man's story, the young miner had thought he was a bit of a nut. He had assumed the shadow train was an illusion caused by heatstroke. Now, with the steady chug-chug-chug growing louder in his ears, the young miner was not so ready to discount the old man's story.

He raised his head again and saw a black speck, dark as the deepest shadow, approaching rapidly. He heard the sharp whistle of a train, once, twice. The speck grew larger, and he could make out the shape of a black steam engine pulling two cars. A yellow headlight gleamed oddly in the white-hot glare of the sun.

The whistle sounded sharply again as the train hurtled toward him. The young miner wanted to leap out of its path, but his body was too far gone. He could not even lift himself. He closed his eyes and braced for impact, but the train slowed suddenly and stopped just a few feet from his head.

A jolly-faced conductor stepped out of the train and came over to him. The conductor bent down and lifted him from the ground. Someone else whom he couldn't see caught his feet,

SHADOW TRAIN

and he was carried inside a passenger car. He felt himself laid down in the aisle, and kind faces surrounded him. "Water," he gasped faintly, just before losing consciousness.

He was wakened by the feeling of cold water being smoothed onto his face. He opened his eyes and saw a tall man wearing a sheriff's badge carefully trickling water from a pitcher over him. The man put down the pitcher and held a cup to his lips, careful not to give him too much at once. The miner had to swish the water around his swollen tongue several times before he could swallow. When he was finally able to speak, he asked the sheriff what had happened.

"Fellow found you nearly dead about five miles out of town," the sheriff answered laconically.

"What town?" asked the young prospector cautiously, visions of shadow trains and jolly conductors in his head.

The sheriff looked at him strangely. "That sun sure must have messed with your head, son, if you can't even remember where you was headed," said the sheriff. "You're in Wilcox, Arizona."

"It's a stop on the train, then?" he asked hesitantly.

"Train? There ain't no train around for miles," said the sheriff. "You'd better have some more water and rest a bit. That sun's nearly sent you loco!"

The young miner laid back down thankfully and closed his eyes. He wasn't sure why the shadow train had come to his rescue, but he was sure glad it had stopped.

26

The Black Cat's Message

I came home late one night after work and found my wife, Ethel, puttering about the kitchen with a big yellow cat at her heels.

"And who is this?" I asked jovially.

"This is our new cat," said Ethel, giving me a hug and a kiss to welcome me home. "She just appeared at the kitchen door and wanted to come in. None of the neighbors know where she came from, so I guess she's ours. It will be nice to have some company around the house."

I bent down and scratched the yellow cat under the chin. She purred and stretched.

"Well, I think our income can stretch far enough to feed three," I said.

My son had taken over my job at the mercantile, and my wife and I were enjoying a leisurely old age. I liked to keep busy, though, and so I spent a few hours every day cutting and hauling wood to be used at the mill.

I went out to milk the cow, and when I came back in, Ethel gave the cat some cream in a saucer.

We sat on the porch after dinner, and the cat sat with us.

"You are a very nice kitty," I said to her. She purred loudly.

"Donald," Ethel said. She sounded worried. I turned to look at her. "The neighbors acted rather oddly when I told them about the cat. They seemed to think she was a ghost or a witch of some sort, transformed into a cat. They told me to get rid of her."

"A witch?" I asked, and laughed heartily. "Are you a witch, little cat?" The cat yawned and stretched. Reluctantly, Ethel started to laugh with me. It seemed such a ludicrous notion. We sat watching the beautiful sunset, then took ourselves to bed.

The cat quickly became an essential part of our household. She would purr us awake each day and wait for cream when I brought in the morning's milking. She followed Ethel around, supervising her work during the day, and sat by the fire at night while we read aloud.

The days became shorter as autumn approached, and often I would work until nearly sunset, cutting and hauling wood. One night in October, I didn't finish hauling my last load until dusk. As soon as I had piled the last log, I started down the road, hoping to get home before dark since I had not brought a lantern with me. I rounded a corner and saw a group of black cats standing in the middle of the road. They were nearly invisible in the growing dark.

As I drew nearer, I saw that they were carrying a stretcher between them. I stopped and rubbed my eyes. That was impossible, my brain told me. But when I looked again, the stretcher was still there, and there was a little dead cat lying on it.

I was astonished. It must be a trick of the light, I thought. Then one of the cats called out, "Sir, please tell Aunt Kan that Polly Grundy is dead."

THE BLACK CAT'S MESSAGE

My mouth dropped open in shock. I shook my head hard, not believing my ears. How ridiculous, I thought. Cats don't talk.

I hurried past the little group, carefully looking the other way. I must be working too hard, I thought. But I couldn't help wondering who Aunt Kan might be. And why did the cat want me to tell her Polly Grundy was dead? Was Polly Grundy the cat on the stretcher?

Suddenly, I was confronted by a small black cat standing directly before me. I stopped and looked down at it. It looked back at me with large green eyes that seemed to glow in the fading light.

"I have a message for Aunt Kan," the cat said. "Tell her that Polly Grundy is dead."

The cat stalked passed me and went to join the other cats grouped around the stretcher.

I was completely nonplussed. This was getting very spooky. Talking cats and a dead Polly Grundy. And who was Aunt Kan? I hurried away as fast as I could walk. Around me, the woods were getting darker and darker. I did not want to stay in those woods with a group of talking cats. Not that I really believed the cats had spoken. It was all a strange, waking dream brought on by too much work.

Behind me, the cats gave a strange shriek and called out together: "Old man! Tell Aunt Kan that Polly Grundy is dead!"

I'd had enough. I sprinted for home as fast as I could go and didn't stop until I had reached the safety of my porch. I paused to catch my breath. I did not want to explain to Ethel that I was seeing and hearing impossible things. She would dose me with caster oil and call the doctor.

When I was sufficiently composed, I went into the house and tried to act normally. I should have known it wouldn't work. Ethel and I had been married for thirty years, and she knew me inside and out. She didn't say anything until after I'd finished the chores. Then she sat me down in front of the fire and brought me my supper. After I'd taken a few bites and started to relax, she said, "Tell me all about it, Donald."

"I don't want to worry you," I said, reluctant to talk about what I had seen and heard on the way home.

The yellow cat was lying by the fire. She looked up when she heard my voice and came to sit by my chair. I offered her a morsel of food, which she accepted daintily.

"I'll worry more if you don't tell me," said Ethel.

"I think maybe something is wrong with my brain," I said slowly. "While I was walking home, I thought I saw some black cats carrying a stretcher with a dead cat on it. Then I thought I heard the cats talking to me. They asked me to tell Aunt Kan that Polly Grundy was dead."

The yellow cat leaped up onto the windowsill. "Polly Grundy is dead?" she cried. "Then I am the Queen of the Witches!"

She switched her tail, and the window flew open with a bang. The yellow cat leaped through it and disappeared into the night, never to return.

Ethel had to dump an entire bucket of water over my head to revive me from my faint.

"The good news," she told me when I sat up, dripping and swearing because the water was ice cold, "is that you have nothing wrong with your brain. The bad news is that our cat has just left us to become the Queen of the Witches. We'll have to get another cat."

"Oh no," I said immediately. "I've had enough of cats."

We got a dog.

27

Tailypo

Way back in the woods of Tennessee lived an old man and his three dogs—Uno, Ino, and Cumptico-Calico. They lived in a small cabin with only one room. This room was their parlor and their bedroom and their kitchen and their sitting room. It had one giant fireplace where the old man cooked supper for himself and his dogs every night.

One night, while the dogs were snoozing by the fire and the old man was washing up after his supper, a very curious creature crept through a crack between the logs of the cabin. The old man stopped washing his plate and stared at the creature. It had a rather round body and the longest tail you ever did see.

As soon as the old man saw that varmint invading his cozy cabin, he grabbed his hatchet. Thwack! He cut off its tail. The creature gave a startled squeak and raced back through the crack in the logs. Beside the fire, the dogs grumbled a bit and rolled over, ignoring the whole thing.

The old man picked up the very long tail. There was some good meat on that tail, so he roasted it over the fire. Cumptico-Calico woke up when she smelled the tail cooking and begged for a bite, but after the old man had his first taste, he couldn't bear to part with a single mouthful. Cumptico-Calico grumbled and lay back down to sleep.

The old man was tired, so he finished washing up and went to bed. He hadn't been sleeping too long when a thumping noise awoke him. It sounded like an animal was climbing up the side of his cabin. He heard a scratch, scratch, scratching noise, like the claws of a cat. And then a voice rang out: "Tailypo, Tailypo; all I want's my Tailypo."

The old man sat bolt upright in bed. He called to the dogs, "Hut! Hut! Hut!" like he did when they were out hunting. Uno and Ino jumped up immediately and began barking like mad. Cumptico-Calico got up slowly and stretched. She was still mad at the old man for not giving her a bite of the tail. The old man sent the dogs outside. He heard them trying to climb the cabin walls after the creature. It gave a squeal and he heard a thump as it jumped to the ground and raced away, the dogs chasing it around the back of the cabin and deep into the woods.

Much later, he heard the dogs return and lay down under the lean-to attached to the cabin. The old man relaxed then and went back to sleep. Along about midnight, the old man woke with his heart pounding madly. He could hear something scratch, scratch, scratching right above his cabin door. "Tailypo, Tailypo; all I want's my Tailypo." The voice was chanting rhythmically against the steady scratch, scratch, scratch at the top of the door.

The old man jumped up, yelling, "Hut! Hut! Hut!" to his dogs. They started barking wildly, and he heard them race around the corner of the house from the lean-to. He saw them catch up with a shadowy something at the gate in front of the cabin. The dogs almost tore the fence down trying to get at it. Finally Cumptico-Calico leapt onto a stump and over the fence, Uno and Ino on her heels, and he heard them chasing the creature way down into the big swamp.

The old man sat up for a while, listening for the dogs to return. About three in the morning, he finally fell asleep again. Toward daybreak, but while it was still dark, the old man was wakened again by the sound of a voice coming from the direction of the swamp. "You know, I know; all I want's my Tailypo." The old man broke out in a cold sweat and yelled, "Hut! Hut! Hut!" for his dogs. But the dogs didn't answer, and the old man feared that the creature had lured them down into the big swamp to kill them. He got out of bed and barricaded the door. Then he hid under the covers and tried to sleep. When it was light, he was going to take his hatchet and his gun and go find his dogs.

Just before morning, the old man was wakened from a fitful doze by a thumping sound right in the cabin. Something was climbing the covers at the foot of his bed. He peered over the covers and saw two pointed ears at the end of the bed. He could hear a scratch, scratch, scratching sound as the creature climbed up the bed, and in a moment he was looking into two big, round, fiery eyes.

The old man wanted to shout for the dogs, but he couldn't make his voice work. He just shivered as the creature crept up the bed toward him. It was large and heavy. He could feel its sharp claws pricking him as it walked up his body. When it reached his face, it bent toward him and said in a low voice, "Tailypo, Tailypo; all I want's my Tailypo."

TAILYPO

All at once, the old man found his voice and he yelled, "I ain't got your Tailypo!" And the creature said, "Yes, you have!" And it grabbed the old man in its claws and tore him to pieces.

The next day, a trapper came across the old man's dogs wandering aimlessly on the other side of the swamp. When the trapper brought the dogs back to the log cabin, he found the old man dead. All that remained were a few scraps of clothing and some grisly bones. As the trapper buried the old man, he heard a faint chuckling sound coming from the swamp, and a voice said, "Now I got my Tailypo." When they heard the voice, the dogs turned tail and ran for their lives.

There's nothing left of that old cabin now except the stone chimney. Folks who live nearby don't like to go there at night, because when the moon is shining brightly and the wind blows across the swamp, sometimes you can still hear a voice saying, "Tailypo."

28

One Last Head

Folks hereabouts were never too fond of the Quick family. Old Man Quick had moved to Michigan territory with his son Bill shortly after the death of his wife. He built a house out back in the woods a long way from the settlement and eked out a living by hunting and trapping. Folks tried to be friendly with Old Man Quick and his boy when they first came to the settlement to sell 'coon skins and buy supplies for the winter. But the hunter and his son weren't much on socializing, and their taciturn ways and rough speech soon turned people against them.

When Bill turned eighteen, things changed a bit. The lad started going to some of the town socials, and he even cracked a few jokes with the fellows playing checkers in the mercantile. Then he started courting a nice young lady from a good family. Bill soon won her heart and her hand, and they settled down with Old Man Quick out in the backwoods. Surprisingly enough, the marriage was a happy one, though the girl's parents disapproved of Bill and were upset that their only daughter lived so far away. When she died in childbirth, her parents swept down upon the grieving father and took their little grandson away with them before he knew what had happened.

After the death of his wife, Bill grew as taciturn as his father and stopped coming in to town. He rarely saw his son and didn't interfere in his upbringing in any way. Things went on like this for years. Then one day Bill came home to find his father dead on the cabin floor. Old Man Quick had been tomahawked to death and partially scalped by an Indian war party that had raided the lonely cabin while Bill was out checking his traps.

Well, Bill just about went mad with grief and fury. And in the years that followed, Bill became even more reclusive. He came to town only once a year for winter supplies, and he rarely communicated with his son, young Tom Quick, who still lived with Bill's in-laws. Bill Quick's cabin became more and more decrepit. The smell coming from it got to be so bad that passing hunters took to avoiding that patch of the woods altogether, opting to make the long trek to town rather than bunking with Bill for the night.

It was during this period that the relationship between the settlement and the local Pottawatomie and Wyandot tribes became strained. No one knew for sure why the tribesmen became so wary of their white neighbors, or why they stopped trading with the people in town. Eventually they withdrew completely, staying close to their tribal lands and avoiding the white men altogether. Things stayed this way for a long time. As the years passed, the townsfolk almost forgot that the settlement had ever traded with the local tribes.

Tom Quick grew into an easygoing young man who was nothing like his taciturn, reclusive father. He'd been much indulged by his maternal grandmother, and he took to drink

and cards rather than hard work and religion. Still, folks preferred him to his father. Bill Quick behaved more and more
like a wild man during his infrequent visits to town. There was
something about him that frightened even the toughest fron-
tiersmen, and something in his eyes that terrified the women-
folk. They claimed time and again that his pupils gleamed red
like those of a maddened beast.

One day, a local hunter passing near Bill Quick's cabin
heard a heart-rending wail coming from inside. He went to
investigate and found Bill Quick lying on a cot in the main
room. Quick begged the hunter to send his son Tom to him
before he died, and the compassionate man hurried into town
to do as Bill bade him.

Tom was surprised and touched by the summons. He had
almost reconciled himself to his father's complete indifference
toward him, though he secretly wished that his father would
love him, if only a little. He hurried through the woods toward
the Quick cabin, hoping to get there before Bill died.

As he entered the clearing where the cabin stood, he was
overwhelmed by the stench of rotting meat. Tom gasped and
reeled backward, retching and fighting to control his stomach.
The smell was far worse than the hunters in town had
described. Tom no longer wondered that they avoided the
place. He wanted to turn and run—but his father was dying
inside that cabin, so he forced himself forward.

He called out to Bill as he knocked on the door, and his
father answered from a cot by the closed door in the far wall. The
smell was even worse inside the cabin, but Tom steeled himself
and stepped into the room. Bill's emaciated, fever-stricken form

lay on the bed. His rough face was flushed with fever, and he was picking restlessly at the tattered cover that lay over him. He snapped at his son to come over where he could see him, and Tom walked slowly to his side. The smell was so bad now that he had to concentrate on controlling his stomach. It seemed to be pulsing out from behind the closed door beside his father's cot.

"I'm dying, curse it," Bill began abruptly when Tom reached the bed, "and I won't be able to finish my life's work. So you're going to have to do it."

"What life's work?" Tom asked. This was the first time the old man had ever spoken of such a thing.

"My revenge!" his father shouted, his pupils gleaming red with madness. "My collection!" Bill gestured toward the closed door and told his son to go into the next room. Trying to breathe only through his mouth, Tom opened the latch and stepped through the door. He was met by a blast of foul air, and he paused in horror as his eyes took in shelf upon shelf of human heads lining every wall of the room. Some were merely skulls; others were half-rotten and crawling with worms and beetles. At least one was nearly fresh, and Tom could still see the look of shock on the face of the Pottawatomie tribesman to whom it had once belonged. There was only one empty space left in the room, at the center of the back wall; a gap just big enough to fit one more head.

"Dear God in heaven!" Tom cried. He backed out of the door, wanting to run but unable to tear his eyes from the grotesque collection.

"Father, what have you done?" he cried, whirling at last to face the dying old man on the cot.

ONE LAST HEAD

"I have avenged your grandfather," Bill Quick said. "On the day he died, I swore to take the heads of 100 Indians in exchange for the scalp they took from my father."

As Tom struggled to listen, Bill described how he tracked down his prey, waiting until he found a tribesman hunting alone and then shooting him through the heart. He never needed more than one bullet for each man, he told his son proudly. And he removed each man's head for his grisly collection. At first, it had been easy to find individual hunters, but the Pottawatomie and Wyandot tribes has become wary as the death toll mounted, and soon none of the men went out hunting alone. But Bill had continued his hunt, stalking his victims ever more carefully, and had continued to add to his terrible collection until this fever had laid him low.

"Ninety-nine heads line my walls," he told his son. "You must kill the last Indian and fulfill my oath to your grandfather."

Fighting to control his revulsion, Tom glared at the figure on the bed and told him that he would have nothing to do with his terrible oath. Bill Quick rose up from his pillow, his eyes red with rage. Tom backed away in horror, afraid that he would become his father's next victim.

"Give me one last head," Bill Quick howled, his voice that of a madman. "One last head!"

Tom ran for the door as fast as his shaking legs would carry him. He fumbled with the latch, hearing the cot creak as his insane father tried to rise. His sweaty palms kept slipping off the metal latch, but finally he got the door open and threw himself into the yard.

The voice of his father followed him as he fled from the Quick cabin: "Fulfill my oath or my spirit will return from the grave to seek you out! One last head!"

Tom ran as far and as fast as he could. When he could run no longer, he flung himself down upon the leaf-strewn dirt and sobbed in fear and rage and revulsion.

Time passed; how long, he didn't know. Finally, when all traces of tears and sickness were gone, he went back to the settlement and straight to the pub to drown his sorrow in whisky.

It took several days and many drinks to ease the horror of Tom's meeting with his father. One evening, the hunter who had brought Tom his father's deathbed message came and told him that the old man had died. He'd checked on him that day and found him dead in his cot. The longer he talked, the harder Tom found it to control his countenance as he visualized every sordid corner of the cabin.

"Don't feel bad that he was alone when he passed, son," the hunter said gruffly, reading only grief in Tom's expression. "Ol' Bill preferred it that way."

Tom nodded wordlessly, and the hunter took himself off, privately touched by the depth of feeling Tom had for his crazy old father.

That night, Tom was awakened by the sound of the wind howling outside his window. He sat up in bed and saw a glow coming from the treetops outside. It formed into the face of his father, his eyes glowing red with insanity, his open mouth a fathomless black hole. "One last head!" the apparition shrieked.

Tom screamed in terror and hid underneath his covers until the ghastly face disappeared. Then he jumped out of bed and ran into the main room to get a bottle of whisky, which he speedily emptied. He spent the rest of the night by the fire, his back to the window, refusing to look up from the flames.

Everywhere he turned the next day, Tom saw his dead father. A pair of red eyes watched as he rode away from the farm toward town. An emaciated form appeared on the roof of the mercantile, glaring down on him as he tied his horse to the hitching post. The wind howled through the main street, whipping around him and shrieking "one last head" into his ear. Tom ended up in the tavern, seeking courage in a bottle, and was so drunk by the day's end that he spent the night in the lock-up.

Tom spent more and more of his time that way, since it seemed the only way to avoid the ghost of his father. But drink only muted the terror he felt when he saw his father's specter lurking in the shadows, or felt malevolent red eyes watching him. And soon, even the voices of other people could not tune out his father's shrieking. "One last head! One last head!"

One night, he told the bartender the whole story, and it became a joke among the townspeople. Every time someone mentioned seeing a Pottawatomie or Wyandot warrior in Tom's presence, folks would nudge one another knowingly. "Here's your chance, Tom," they would say. "Better go get him now, before your father's ghost returns!"

Tom's life became one of sheer misery. He couldn't hold a job because of his drinking, and he was teased and tormented constantly by the wags in town over his father's curse. Just when Tom thought things couldn't get any worse, he was visited at midnight by the rotting corpse of his father. Bill Quick stood in the doorway, his maggot-ridden skeleton and shredding skin clear as day in the bright moonlight. The specter held a hunting rifle in one hand and a knife in the other. Pointing the rifle at his cowering son, Bill Quick made his demand. "Ninety-nine heads line my walls! You must kill one last Indian and fulfill my oath to your grandfather!"

Tom was so terrified he couldn't speak. He backed away until his shoulders hit the wall behind him. His body was shaking uncontrollably. He wanted to flee, but he stood frozen in place, unable to take his eyes off the demented figure in the doorway.

"One last head!" the corpse shrieked, a piece of its lip dropping off as it howled. "I need one last head. You have until midnight, or the spirit of your murdered grandfather will return with me, and you will answer to him."

Tom's courage broke, and with it went his mind. With a shriek every bit as horrible as that of his father, he dove out the window and ran toward the settlement. His screams of terror woke the whole town. He leapt from house to house, pounding on the wooden doors until they buckled, babbling insanely about his father's specter, and begging someone, anyone, to take him in. The good people of the town barred their doors, and the townsmen ran him off with rifles, fearing that the drunken madman might harm their women and children.

Tom was last seen plunging into the woods in the direction of his father's cabin. When the townsmen went to check on him the next day, they found his house empty. Taking their rifles, they started a careful search, not sure what would happen when they found the poor, insane drunk. They followed his trail easily through the woods, but the tracks disappeared just inside the clearing where the Quick cabin stood.

The air still reeked of rotting flesh. To the right of the cabin, Bill Quick's grave lay undisturbed in the flickering afternoon light. The searchers approached the cabin reluctantly, covering their noses before they entered. The main room was empty and showed signs of long abandonment. The dirt floor showed no new tracks, but there was still the back room to check.

One man crossed to the door and pulled it open. The stench of rotten flesh bellowed out into the room. Gagging desperately, the man stepped through the door and gave a cry of terror that brought the other searchers running. They were instantly overwhelmed by the grisly sight of rotting human heads lining the shelves in the room. But it was the bulging eyes and agony-twisted face of the latest victim that held their attention. Filling the one hundredth space at the center of the back wall was the head of Tom Quick. The rest of his body was never found.

29

Dark Passenger

She boarded the ship in Buffalo, a small, delicate figure wearing the black clothes of deep mourning with a dark veil obscuring most of her beautiful white features. The woman had contacted the brig's captain unexpectedly, requesting a special late-season charter to take her west. There was quite a lot of money involved, and as a bonus, the captain had found a shipment of whisky to sell in Chicago. So he accepted the charter and told the first mate to round up an impromptu crew—not so easy at the end of the season.

The first mate caught a flash of the passenger's luminous black eyes in the twilight as she cautioned the men carrying her luggage to handle it with care. Along with several large suitcases, there was a curious chest about five feet long, two feet wide, and two feet thick that had startled the first mate. He had never seen anything quite like it. The sight of the chest made him shudder, as if a sliver of ice had pierced straight through his heart. The box looked almost like a coffin. But that was nonsense.

Feeling his gaze, the woman whirled to look at him. For a moment, he caught another glimpse of her beautiful pale face beneath the obscuring veil. The steady catlike gleam in her eyes made him lose his breath momentarily. She had the sharp gaze of a hunter, and he did not like the way she looked him up and down, her eyes lingering at the open collar of his shirt. The first mate nodded nervously to her, touching the brim of his cap. Then he turned away to supervise the loading of the barrels into the hold of the brig. Out of the corner of his eye, he saw the captain offer the woman his arm to escort her to his cabin. She leaned heavily against it, as if the short journey to the dock had fatigued her. It was puzzling behavior, considering the swiftness with which she had turned to gaze upon him.

As they prepared to set sail, the first mate pondered their strange passenger. According to the cabin boy, she had insisted that the large chest be stowed in her room and had made the boy rearrange the furnishings until it fit. The cabin boy had been much taken by her beauty. He kept chattering to the sailors about how kind she was and how pretty she was too, if perhaps a little pale. The boy thought she had been ill, and he supposed she must be taking the sudden voyage for the sake of her health. The first mate was not so sure. A trip along the Great Lakes during the summer months might have been pre-scribed, but what doctor would send his patient on a lakes voy-age in the late fall, when the air was cold, the water freezing, and terrible storms ever loomed on the horizon?

The first mate soon forgot the dark passenger as a tug towed them to the mouth of the harbor and they set sail westward. He kept a sharp eye on the men, none of whom he knew very well. They were sailing with a limited crew—just the captain, himself, the cook, the ship's boy, and the five men forward. None of the men were part of the regular ship's complement, and so the mate watched closely to make sure they did their jobs.

A strong northeast breeze blew up and kept them sailing well, though the lake grew choppy in the morning. The woman did not appear all day—a fact the first mate attributed to seasickness. The cook mentioned rapping on her door with an offering of tea and biscuits, but he had received no answer.

Toward dusk, the first mate realized that he hadn't seen the cabin boy since the previous evening. He casually questioned the crew, cook, and captain, but no one knew where the boy had gone. A search was made of the entire ship, but it seemed the boy had disappeared into thin air. It was finally determined that he had fallen overboard during the night, and this fact was entered into the ship's log.

After sundown, the woman appeared on deck and inquired about the cabin boy, whom she had not seen since the previous night. The captain sadly informed her of the boy's fate. She took the news stoically and stood at the rail for a long while, looking over the dark waters. Later, when the captain casually asked about her health, she told him she felt queasy and declined dinner. Still, the first mate noticed that she appeared stronger after her long rest, and that a little color had come into her pale cheeks. After one or two attempts at conversation, which were politely rebuffed, he left the dark passenger alone. But something about her puzzled him, and he kept an eye on her while he worked.

Finally, instructing the wheelman to call him if the weather changed, the first mate went down to his cabin to get some sleep. An hour later, he was awakened abruptly by the violent

DARK PASSENGER

rolling of the ship. Cursing the wheelman for not informing him of an approaching storm, he rushed to the deck. To his astonishment, he found the wheelman in a daze and rocking unsteadily at the wheel. With an oath, the first mate grabbed the wheel and turned the ship, shoving the wheelman aside in his haste. The wheelman had a good reputation at the Buffalo docks, but as far as the first mate was concerned, his actions were that of a landlubber. Drunk at the wheel! If the weather had been bad, they could all have been killed.

A moment later the captain appeared along with several members of the crew. The first mate set another man to the wheel and bent to check the breath of the former wheelman. Oddly, the first mate smelled no alcohol, a fact confirmed by the captain. Sudden illness must have been the cause of the wheelman's grave error. The captain ordered the ailing man below deck. So unsteady on his feet was he that two of the sailors had to carry him to his hammock.

They caught a good wind just before dawn and sailed quickly across Lake Erie, arriving near Colchester Reef at dusk. There was no sign of the dark passenger all day, though the lake was smooth and clear and the bright sun made the trip a pleasure. The first mate wondered why she stayed below deck, but work kept him too busy to ponder for long; they were shorthanded due to the strange illness of the former wheelman.

The captain elected to spend the night topside as the ship was entering the dangerous waters leading up to the Detroit River. The first mate enjoyed a good night's rest and went to relieve the captain just before dawn, around the time a tugboat stopped alongside to give them a hawser for the tow up the river. The captain reported a calm night and nothing out of the ordinary, save for a short visit from the dark-haired woman around midnight.

As the captain prepared to go below, the gleaming rays of the rising sun illuminated a figure huddled on the foredeck. The captain and first mate ran forward and found a second stricken crewman. He was as pale as the former wheelman, and his eyes were dazed. They got him below deck and the captain gave him some medicine from their supply box. The first mate was grim as he took command of the watch. Two men were sick and the cabin boy drowned—what an ill-fated journey!

The ship dropped the tow line at dusk and continued out onto Lake Huron under a steady breeze. The first mate thanked his lucky stars that the weather had remained fine. He did not relish the notion of being shorthanded during a lake hurricane. When night fell, the dark passenger came up on deck. She wore no veil this evening, and the first mate could see her beautiful face clearly for the first time. It was evident that the lake air agreed with her, for there was a flush of health and color in her cheeks, and her lips were red and full. She gave a cold response to his greeting, and her steely hunter's eyes narrowed as she took him in. The first mate repressed a shiver. Beautiful she might be, but this was a woman whom he would never voluntarily approach.

The next morning, the cook fell ill with the same strange disease that had struck the two crewmen. The captain ordered him to bed, and the crewmen had to make do with their own meager cooking skills. There was no sign of the woman during the day, and no response when the first mate knocked on her door to ask if she would like some stew.

At dusk, the captain retired below deck for a short break, but failed to return topside. The first mate stomped on the deck above his cabin, the signal they had arranged when the captain was needed above, but there was no response. With a sinking heart, the mate went below and found the captain white as a sheet, with dazed eyes and a lethargic air—the symptoms of the illness that was devastating the crew. The first mate doused him with a tonic from their rapidly depleting medical supply and sent one of the healthy crewmembers to sit with the ill man.

Assuming temporary command of the ship, the first mate remained on deck until nearly 3 A.M. The dark passenger appeared once around midnight to take in the air, and the first mate was amazed by the change in her appearance. She was glowing with health—her face flushed pink, her lips dark red, her eyes sparkling. But he found her beauty strangely repulsive, as if it had been bought at a great price, though he scarcely knew what he meant by the thought.

The cook was dead in the morning. The exhausted crewman who had been attending the ill men had fallen asleep just before dawn. He awakened to find the cook as white as a sheet, as if he had been drained of all his blood, with no life or breath in him. The crewman summoned the first mate from his bunk, where he had retreated to get a few hours of sleep. The first mate stared at the dead cook in sorrow and perplexity. He had never seen a disease before that would deprive a man of so much blood. To check, the mate stuck the blade of his knife into the cook's arm, and received only a hint of redness where there should have been a spurt of blood. Together, the men wrapped up the cook's body and placed it in the hold.

They headed into the Straits and came abeam of Old Mission Light after dark. The woman appeared late in the evening, and the first mate was astonished to see that she was dressed in all white. She looked exquisitely lovely in the pale moonlight, and she seemed to glide rather than walk as she walked about the deck, eventually moving forward until she disappeared into the darkness before the foremast. Noticing the weary air of the man at the wheel, the mate sent him below to get some rest, taking the wheel himself. The woman passed him by in silence a few minutes later, and he saw her no more that night.

The next morning, another crewmember was found collapsed on the foredeck, claimed by the mysterious disease that had killed the cook. That left two healthy men and the mate to keep the ship on course for Chicago. The mate grimly considered his options. They could just barely manage to reach their destination if the weather remained fair. Given their current location, there was no good place to dock, even if he had wished it. The mate decided to stay the course as long as possible, though he could no longer spare a man to watch over the sick or cook for the passenger.

The storm struck suddenly, with no warning. One moment there was a clear blue sky, and the next the brig was rocking violently in the waves, and the wind had blown out the foretopsail. The first mate was more glad than sorry at the loss, for they were too shorthanded to bring it in. But the fierce wind was not done with the brig. The next heavy gust took both the mainsail and the foresail, and a third ripped off the forestaysail. The ship rolled and pitched under them, but with the poles bared, the mate and his two remaining crewmen managed to get her back under control. When the ship was stabilized, the mate left both hands manning the wheel and slipped below the gyrating deck to secure the safety of the passenger and the captain.

The first mate knocked loudly on the woman's door and shouted so as to be heard above the roar of the storm. There was no response. Alarmed by her silence, he thrust the door open, afraid that she had been injured, but he found the room empty. The strange chest lay open on the floor, bare of all, save a few inches of dirt. Behind the lid protruded a small leg. Steadying himself against the roll of the ship, the first mate staggered forward and slammed down the lid of the chest. Behind it was the dead body of the little cabin boy. He was as pale as the moon, obviously drained of all blood—just like the cook had been. The mate was puzzled and alarmed. What was the boy doing here, in the dark passenger's cabin?

He returned to the rocking passageway and carefully made his way to the captain's door. Thrusting it open, the mate's eyes immediately fell on a horrible scene. The captain lay on the floor, the dark-haired woman leaning over him. She was drinking his blood. The dark passenger's hearing must have been superb, for she whirled at once upon his entry, her mouth dripping red and her fierce hunter's eyes gleaming with an unholy light. With a shout of horror, the mate leapt backward out of the cabin.

The woman rose with uncanny speed, but a sudden lurch of the storm-tossed ship threw her to the deck and knocked the mate into a bulwark. He recovered quickly, being used to the extreme movements of a storm, and ran up the ramp to the quarterdeck. Topside, he saw at once that the wheel had been smashed and the two crewmen swept overboard. Lightning flashed, thunder rumbled, and the downpour drenched him as the mate staggered forward, his eyes on the massive, straining masts. The ship was rolling terribly in the waves, and the first mate knew they were all doomed.

Then the woman struck him from behind, knocking him to the deck against the mainmast fife rail. The mate rolled over and looked up in horror at the exquisitely beautiful, evil figure towering above him in the dim light of the storm, realizing at last that the dark passenger was the source of the fatal illness that had struck down his entire crew. Her ragged white dress, stained with the captain's blood, was flapping in the wind. Her long black hair was loose and streamed behind her. Her predator's eyes gleamed red with bloodlust as she stalked the mate across the heaving deck—taking her time so as to enjoy every expression of terror on his face. He could see two fangs thrusting down over her glowing red lips as she picked him up with incredible strength and opened her mouth for the fatal bite.

But a sudden roll of the ship loosened her grip, and the slap of a huge wave over the deck drove her back a few feet. The first mate gripped the rail desperately, praying to whomever would listen for a miracle. With a tremendous thunderclap, a bolt of lightning struck the main topmast directly above them. It shattered, raining down huge splinters of wood. One long spear struck the woman right through the heart, pinning her to the deck. Clinging to the rail in profound shock, the mate stared at the evil creature as blood spilled out over the deck, to be immediately washed away by the rain and the slap of the waves. The woman, whoever—or whatever—she was, was dead.

Then the ship tipped up, slipped back, and capsized, throwing the mate into the chilly waters of the lake. Surfacing almost immediately, he grabbed hold of a floating hatch grate and hung on while the ship slid below the surface. He was still drifting hours later when the storm abated, and he was nearly dead from cold and exhaustion when the lake threw him up onto one of the islands.

Luckily, the mate was found by a fisherman and taken in. When he had recovered enough to tell his tale, he cautiously reported a sudden storm that capsized his ship. The mate made no mention of the strange illness of the crew and its probable cause. Who would believe him, anyway?

The wreck went unremarked and unlamented, for which the mate was glad. No one in Chicago had any interest in the ship, which was uninsured and had belonged solely to her dead captain. The makeshift crew had been composed of drifters who had no families to speak of. As for the dark passenger, the mate was unwilling to pursue any inquiries regarding her family and friends, lest he meet another such creature as the one that had taken the life of the crew. Instead, the mate left the matter to the indifferent jurisdiction of the shipping authorities and went back east to take up a position in his father's firm. He never sailed on the Great Lakes again.

30

Bloody Mary

I finished pounding the nail into the horseshoe and carefully set the horse's hoof down onto the floor. The mare shifted her weight gratefully back onto all four feet and sighed deeply. I patted her flank, then put my tools down and led her into the small stall I kept next to the smithy for the use of my customers. She settled down quickly and began pulling at the hay in the rack.

"Papa," I heard a small voice call from behind me. I turned and smiled when I saw my only daughter, my sweet little Emily. With her cornflower blue eyes and long golden braids, she was the image of her mother. Emily had a deep basket hanging from her little arm. Even from here, I could smell roast chicken and sage-and-onion stuffing. My favorite.

"Mama asked me to bring you lunch, since you have such a busy schedule today," Emily said. She carried the basket into the smithy and set it onto a low table. "She sent extra so I could have lunch with you," she added with a grin that revealed a missing front tooth. I grinned back and bowed her into a chair.

We sat munching the good food and talking about which animals I had seen today and who needed what metalwork done around town. *Thump, thump, thump.* Emily's small feet bounced against the leg of the chair as we talked together.

172

Suddenly the thumping stopped, and Emily's blue eyes grew large. She was staring out into the yard, and I saw her tremble. I turned at once, wanting to see what had upset her.

An old crone with a cruel, wrinkled face and long, straggly white hair stood in the yard, leaning heavily on a cane. It was Bloody Mary. Or rather, it was Frau Gansmueller, I should have said. Bloody Mary was a nickname the children had given the old woman long ago. They thought she was a witch and were frightened by her.

Frau Gansmueller lived deep in the forest in a tiny cottage and sold herbal remedies for a living. None of the good folk living in town dared to cross the old crone for fear that their cows would go dry, their food stores rot away before winter, their children take sick of fever, or any number of terrible things that an angry witch could do to her neighbors.

I stepped hastily into the yard and sketched a bow to the old woman. "How may I be of service, Frau Gansmueller?" I asked quickly. Bloody Mary glared at me with narrow, coal-black eyes.

"I've come for an andiron, Herr Smith," she said in her soft, sibilant voice. I repressed a shiver at the soft hissing tone. Her voice sounded like that of a talking snake.

"Fine, fine," I stammered. I hurried inside, motioned to Emily to stay where she was, and brought out a new andiron for the old crone. I handed it to her, naming a sum half of what it was worth. I wasn't taking any chances on upsetting the old witch. She examined it critically before putting it into her basket next to the small mirror she always carried. Then she counted out the money into my hand.

BLOODY MARY

As she turned to leave, Bloody Mary stopped suddenly, glancing back into the smithy. "What a pretty little girl you have, Herr Smith," she said, offering Emily a crooked smile and stroking the small mirror in her basket. Emily turned white with fear and smiled back.

"Thank you, Frau Gansmueller," I said as politely as I could. She hobbled away then, and I watched her until she disappeared around a bend in the road. A moment later, a small hand crept into mine, and Emily said, "I do not like her, Papa."

"Neither do I, child," I said. Then a stab of fear went through my heart. What would Bloody Mary do to Emily if she ever heard the child saying such things about her? I added, "But we must always be polite to her, Emily, and never speak unkindly about her. Promise me that you will always be polite and kind."

Emily looked deeply into my eyes and nodded solemnly. "I promise, Papa," she said, and I knew she would keep her word. We finished our meal in silence, then Emily took the basket home to her mama.

It was about a week after the incident at the smithy that the first little girl went missing from our town. Little Rosa, the daughter of the shoemaker, disappeared from her home in the middle of the night. She was just a wee mite of a girl who rarely ever left her yard. A search party was formed. We scoured the woods, the local buildings, and all the houses and barns, but there was no sign of the missing girl. Her mother sat and rocked in a corner all day, clutching her daughter's favorite doll and saying nothing. No one could comfort her.

Then the buxom twelve-year-old daughter of Franklin Taylor went for a walk in the woods with a few friends and did not come home. Her girlfriends looked everywhere but could not find her. Another search party was formed, and we examined every tree, every meadow, every stream, to no avail. A few brave souls even went to Bloody Mary's cottage in the woods to see if the witch had taken the girl, but she denied any knowledge of the disappearance.

Next it was Theresa, the brown-eyed, eight-year-old daughter of the basketmaker who went to fetch groceries from the mercantile and did not return. Again we searched, and again the girl remained missing. Everyone in town was frantic with fear. The young girls were instructed to walk in pairs and never to go out without letting their parents know about it. Of course, Bloody Mary was at the back of everyone's mind. Who else but a witch could make three young girls disappear so completely? But there was no proof, and no one dared to say anything.

During the hunt for young Theresa, Bloody Mary had insisted that the girl's father come into her house and search it, so that no suspicion should attach itself to her. The cottage was completely normal save for a fancy mirror on the kitchen wall next to the fireplace, a strange luxury for a poor woman's house. Stranger still was the way the mirror sometimes reflected things that weren't there. The basketmaker glimpsed his house in the village within the glass as he turned away from his examination of the fireplace chimney, but when he walked over to look in the mirror, it reflected only his face and the room behind it. Not surprisingly, the basketmaker found nothing else in the cottage or grounds of Bloody Mary to connect her with his daughter's disappearance.

My wife was keeping Emily in the house all the time now. Only the boys went to the schoolhouse each day, while my wife tutored Emily at home. Sometimes, as I worked at the lathe or hammered hot horseshoes, I remembered Bloody Mary looking into the smithy at Emily and telling me what a pretty child she was. In those moments, I would shiver uncontrollably, unable to warm myself in spite of the heat pouring off the hot smithy fire.

"Herr Smith," a sibilant voice calling from the smithy doorway broke into my thoughts. I knew that voice. It was Bloody Mary. I turned to look at the crone and bit my lip to keep from exclaiming aloud in amazement. Her haggard appearance had changed dramatically. She looked younger and much more attractive.

"How may I be of service, Frau Gansmueller?" I asked, laying down my hammer and tongs.

"I need some new pothooks," Bloody Mary said, her black eyes snapping at me with a malicious amusement that made my hands shake with fear. I drew in a deep breath before I fetched some pothooks for her. Again, I named a low price, and again she examined them carefully before paying me.

"Say good day from me to your mistress and your pretty young daughter," Bloody Mary said, fingering the mirror in her basket thoughtfully. Then she gave me a wicked smile and turned away with a rather flirtatious flick of her long skirts. I swallowed hard as I watched her leave. Her reference to Emily frightened me badly.

As soon as I could, I closed the shop and hurried home. To my relief, I found Emily studying her books in the corner, her blond head bent industriously over her work. My wife looked up from her cooking in surprise at my early arrival. I took her aside and told her about Bloody Mary's visit. She gasped, and her body started trembling uncontrollably. I took her into my arms, and we clung together for a long time. Then we discussed the matter and decided that the child would have to go and stay with her grandmother until the crisis had passed. Until arrangements could be made, one of us would have to be with her at every moment of the day. With this decided, we went and broke the news to Emily and her brothers.

I lay awake late into the night, praying for the safety of my little girl.

Just after I dozed off, I was awakened by my wife. She had a sore tooth and was finding it hard to lie on her right side. She motioned me back to sleep and went downstairs to find the herbal remedy given to her by the apothecary.

I was awakened for the second time by soft strains of music that seemed to be coming from everywhere and nowhere at the same time. Even as I listened, the eerie, luring melody faded away. And then I heard my wife screaming.

I jumped out of bed and ran downstairs. My wife was racing out the front door, her blue eyes fixed on a small, barefooted figure clad in a white nightdress that was walking toward the edge of town. It was Emily! I leaped passed my wife and ran to intercept my daughter. Emily was in a trance, a happy smile on her face, her eyes glazed. She must be hearing the same music that had awakened me.

I caught her in my arms, but she pulled away immediately and continued walking toward the edge of town and the dark woods beyond. I was shocked. Emily was a tiny girl, but she had thrust my work-hardened blacksmith's body away as if I were a stripling. I ran forward and grabbed hold of her again, bracing my body as she struggled against me. My wife wrapped her arms around my waist, holding on tightly and screaming for help.

Her desperate cries woke our neighbors, and they came to assist us in our struggle. Lights went on everywhere as the townsfolk realized that another child was in trouble. Suddenly, a sharp-eyed lad gave a shout and pointed toward a strange light at the edge of the woods.

Leaving my wife and the other women to restrain Emily, I led the men toward the mysterious light. As we entered the field just outside the woods, we saw Bloody Mary standing beside a large oak tree, holding her small mirror in one hand and a magic wand in the other. The wand was pointed toward my house, and reflected in the mirror was the beautiful young face of my daughter. Bloody Mary was glowing with an unearthly radiance as she set her evil spell upon Emily.

Many of the men who had responded to my wife's screams had the forethought to bring guns and pitchforks. One of them thrust a gun into my hand as we ran toward the witch. "It has silver bullets," he shouted to me. I nodded grimly. Silver bullets were the only kind that could kill a witch.

When she heard the commotion, Bloody Mary broke off her spell and fled back into the woods. I stopped, took aim with the gun, and shot at her. The bullet hit Bloody Mary in the hip, and she fell to the ground. Immediately, angry townsmen swarmed upon her, pulling her to her feet and carrying her back into the field. Grimly, I picked up the wand and the mirror that had fallen into the dirt and leaves when I shot their owner.

The judge, who had been the first neighbor to arrive on the scene when we tried to restrain the entranced Emily, quickly pronounced Bloody Mary guilty of witchcraft, kidnapping, and the murder of the three missing girls. He sentenced her to death at the stake, and the townsmen immediately built a huge bonfire, right there in the field. They tied the witch and her magic wand to the wood and set it ablaze. I smashed the magic hand mirror myself.

As she burned, Bloody Mary glared at us through the flames. Staring straight into my eyes, she screamed a curse against all of us. "If anyone," she cried, "mentions my name aloud before a mirror, I will send my spirit to them and will revenge myself upon them in payment for my death!" The witch pointed her hand toward the shards of glass at my feet as she spoke. For a moment they glowed blue, then faded again into darkness.

Many who heard the curse shuddered and stepped back from the fire, but I stood as still as stone and watched as the evil woman paid for her black deeds. When she was dead, I led the villagers to her house in the woods, where we smashed her other magic mirror. With the destruction of the mirror, the concealment spell on the cottage lifted, and we soon found the unmarked graves of the little girls the evil witch had murdered and buried underneath the woodpile. According to the records she kept, she had created a spell that used their blood to make her young again.

So the lives of the other young girls in town were spared, and my Emily was safe at last. My daughter grew into a beautiful young woman who married the minister's son and had three children of her own. But Bloody Mary's curse also lived, if only in rumor. Tales have been told of young people who were foolish enough to chant Bloody Mary's name before a darkened mirror, and so summoned the vengeful spirit of the witch. It is said that the witch tore the poor victims' bodies to pieces and ripped their souls from their mutilated flesh, trapping them forever in burning torment inside the mirror with her. Having seen the witch at work, I find I cannot discount the tales, though I myself have never tried it.

Resources

Asfar, Dan. *Ghost Stories of Michigan*. Edmonton, AB: Ghost House Publishing, 2002.

Battle, Kemp P. *Great American Folklore*. New York: Doubleday & Company, Inc., 1986.

Botkin, B. A., ed. *A Treasury of American Folklore*. New York: Crown, 1944.

———. *A Treasury of New England Folklore*. New York: Crown Publishers, Inc., 1965.

———. *A Treasury of Railroad Folklore*. New York: Crown, 1953.

———. *A Treasury of Southern Folklore*. New York: Crown Publishers, 1949.

Brewer, J. Mason. *American Negro Folklore*. Chicago, IL: Quadrangle Books, 1972.

Brunvand, Jan Harold. *The Choking Doberman and Other Urban Legends*. New York: W. W. Norton, 1984.

———. *Folklore in America*. New York: Doubleday & AMP, 1966.

———. *Folklore from the Working Folk of America.* New York: Doubleday, 1973.

———. *The Vanishing Hitchhiker.* New York: W. W. Norton, 1981. Coffin, Tristram P., and Hennig Cohen, eds.

Cohen, Daniel. *Ghostly Tales of Love & Revenge.* New York: Putnam Publishing Group, 1992.

Cohen, Daniel, and Susan Cohen. *Hauntings & Horrors.* New York: Dutton Children's Books, 2002.

Cornplanter, J. J. *Legends of the Longhouse.* Philadelphia: J. B. Lippincott, 1938.

Dorson, R. M. *America in Legend.* New York: Pantheon Books, 1973.

Editors of Life. *The Life Treasury of American Folklore.* New York: Time Inc., 1961.

Erdoes, Richard, and Alfonso Ortiz. *American Indian Myths and Legends.* New York: Pantheon Books, 1984.

Flanagan, J. T., and A. P. Hudson. *The American Folk Reader.* New York: A. S. Barnes & Co., 1958.

Hallenbeck, Cleve, and J. H. William. *Legends of the Spanish Southwest.* Glendale, CA: Arthur H. Clark Company, 1938.

Jones, Louis C. *Things That Go Bump in the Night.* New York: Hill and Wang, 1959.

Leach, M. *The Rainbow Book of American Folk Tales and Legends.* New York: The World Publishing Co., 1958.

Leeming, David, and Jake Page. *Myths, Legends, & Folktales of America*. New York: Oxford University Press, 1999.

Peck, Catherine, ed. *A Treasury of North American Folk Tales*. New York: W. W. Norton, 1998.

Pitkin, David J. *Ghosts of the Northeast*. New York: Aurora Publications, 2002.

Polley, J., ed. *American Folklore and Legend*. New York: Reader's Digest Association, 1978.

Reevy, Tony. *Ghost Train!* Lynchburg, VA: TLC Publishing, 1998.

Schwartz, Alvin. *Scary Stories to Tell in the Dark*. New York: Harper Collins, 1981.

Skinner, Charles M. *American Myths and Legends, Vol. 1*. Philadelphia: J. B. Lippincott, 1903.

———. *Myths and Legends of Our Own Land, Vol. 2*. Philadelphia: J. B. Lippincott, 1896.

Smith, Barbara. *Ghost Stories of California*. Renton, WA: Lone Pine Publishing, 2000.

Spence, Lewis. *North American Indians: Myths and Legends Series*. London: Bracken Books, 1985.

Stonehouse, Frederick. *Haunted Lakes*. Duluth, MN: Lake Superior Port Cities, Inc., 1997.

———. *Haunted Lakes II*. Duluth, MN: Lake Superior Port Cities, Inc., 2000.

Thompson, Harold W. *New York State Folktales, Legends, and Ballads*. New York: Dover Publications, Inc., 1939.

Wilson, Patty A. *The Pennsylvania Ghost Guide, Vol. I*. Waterfall, PA: Piney Creek Press, 2000.

Young, Richard, and Judy Dockery. *Ghost Stories from the American Southwest*. Little Rock, AR: August House Publishers, 1991.

Zeitlin, Steven J., Amy J. Kotkin, and Holly Cutting Baker. *A Celebration of American Family Folklore*. New York: Pantheon Books, 1982.

About the Author

S. E. Schlosser has been telling stories since she was a child, when games of "let's pretend" quickly built themselves into full-length tales acted out with friends. A graduate of Houghton College, the Institute of Children's Literature, and Rutgers University, she created and maintains the award-winning Web site Americanfolklore.net, where she shares a wealth of stories from all fifty states, some dating back to the origins of America. Sandy spends much of her time answering questions from visitors to the site. Many of her favorite e-mails come from other folklorists who delight in practicing the old tradition of who can tell the tallest tale.